Awaken the Mind

Awaken the Mind

Communion with Sean Liburd

The Sharing of Thoughts and Emotions,
An Intimate Communication Between a People

To order additional copies of this book, contact:
Xlibris Corporation
1-888-795-4274
www.Xlibris.com
Orders@Xlibris.com
43980

Contents

DEDICATION

To the beauty, strength, and spirit of Mother Africa's children.

Expression of Gratitude

Creator of all life, I recognize and exalt your presence in this time and place.
I give thanks for the breath of life.
Creator of all life, I understand that I am a product of those who came before me.
I give thanks for all my ancestors, including those who died so that I could live and those who chose to live, leaving me their example.
Creator of all life, I am aware of the invaluable guidance provided by my chosen guardians in this physical realm.
I give thanks for my parents: Horace and Girlie Liburd.
I give thanks for Linnette and Veronica Liburd, my sisters, who have been my mothers.
Creator of all life, I acknowledge my siblings for their contributions to my being.
I give thanks for my sisters: Julie, Juta, Michele, Myrna, Sandra, Carol, and Doris.
I give thanks for my brothers: Tony, Clayton, Alison, Andy, Kenneth, Nigel, Gene, Floris, and Orville.
Creator of all life, you have assured a bountiful harvest.
I give thanks for my plethora of nieces and nephews.
Creator of all life, one came forth to be at my side providing support and encouragement.
I give thanks for my friend, business partner, and wife, Carolette Liburd.
Creator of all life, you have surrounded me with feminine energy.
I give thanks for Joanne.
I give thanks for Alana.
I give thanks for Rochele.
I give thanks for Camille.
I give thanks for Jurrene.
Creator of all life, I am counting my blessings.
I am thankful for all who have been a part of my heart.
I am thankful for all who have blessed me with love, beauty, and lessons.
I am thankful for the journey and every being that has traveled along with me, serving purpose.
Creator of all life, I am thankful.

Introduction

When we look at the word *communion*, it can be defined as the sharing of interests or thoughts among a particular group of people. It is fellowship. It is a meeting of minds and souls in consecration. This term *communion* is the joining of two powerful words. The first, *commune*, can be described as a group of people who share a space or accommodation. It also speaks of being intimate, in close relation to a thing or a people. The second word, *union*, can denote a whole formed from many parts or members. When a couple chooses to embark upon matrimony, it is called a union. Thus a union is sacred or holy.

The words *commune* and *union* do have similar definitions; however, when joined together, they convey a sense of love and camaraderie: brotherhood and sisterhood. Where these are present, you have community. When people gather together, they are connecting to the power within themselves; and through this connection, they learn to know themselves and know each other. Essentially, it is the communion with your community which reveals who you are and who you could be.

How fitting it is that Sean Liburd has become the catalyst for the community and its communion. Whether through his business, Knowledge Bookstore—which continues to attract souls eager to reunite with each other and share a spiritual union—or through the pages of this book, which will connect like-minded readers with anecdotes, commentaries, inspirational thoughts, and instructions integral to the community's survival.

Just as Knowledge Bookstore has become the meeting place for the community, this book is the meeting place for our collective spirit. We can relate to one another through these words, which convey the relationship that the community has and could have in the future. Sean's book is a call to remember ourselves. That is to recollect our original way of thinking, to bring prodigal sons and daughters back to the fold, and to practice rituals which have long been forgotten. *Awaken the Mind: Communion with Sean Liburd* gives us an opportunity to grow and understand self. This is a very pivotal moment in our history, for we have the opportunity to begin *building* and to *redefine* our *community*. To expose our true selves and *culture* as one that is *naked*. We will *manifest* our *spirituality* by *honoring our ancestors* and use *the power of thought* for *nation building.* We will remember *to be African* and be proud of our *African-centered education.*

Kevin "Heron" Jones
Brampton, ON
November 2007

Kevin "Heron" Jones is a writer, spoken-word recording artist, storyteller, and journalist. He is the author of a book of poems entitled *I Am a Child of the Sun* (PoeticSoul). His poetry is also featured in *T-Dot Griots: An anthology of Toronto's Black Storytellers* (Trafford).

African-centered Education

Nea onnim no sua a, ohu.
   "He who does not know can know from learning."
   Symbol of knowledge, life long education, and continued quest for knowledge.

Reading

You should read at least four hours a day. The best time to read is in the evening after you have retired from work and after you have rested and before sleeping hours, but do so before morning, so that during your sleeping hours what you have read may become subconscious, that is to say, planted in your memory. Never go to bed without doing some reading.

—Taken from *Message to the People: The Course of African Philosophy* by Marcus Garvey

What madness! "The Honorable Marcus Garvey must have really had a lot of free time on his hands to be able to read four hours a day, there is just not enough time in a day . . . with all my responsibilities . . . this system just won't allow me the opportunity to . . . . how is reading going to help me pay the bills?" We make time for things that we truly want in life! Many of us believe the events that happen in our lives and how we use our time is outside our control. They are not unless we allow them to be. Marcus Garvey was committed and focused on developing solutions to the plight of African people. He was self-educated and understood the importance of taking responsibility for your own self-development. As the founder and leader of the Universal Negro Improvement Association (UNIA), Marcus Garvey created an organization dedicated to unite all Africans, to encourage the spirit of self-love, to lend a helping hand when a brother or sister is down, to create self-reliance, and to reclaim Africa. We are each unique beings with the ability to contribute to the growth of humanity in a positive manner. Brother Marcus serves as an example of what can be achieved when the mind and heart work in unison. In trying to recover my memories, I understand his message about the importance of reading. I will continue to read to the children, to my elders, to my peers, and to myself. I will read for pleasure, stimulation, inspiration, knowledge, understanding, experience, and to awaken my mind to the Divine.

The Power of Reading

Reading gave me hope. For me it was the open door.

—Oprah Winfrey

Not so long ago, African people who were brought to the Americas and the Caribbean as slaves were forbidden to read. Have you ever asked yourself why? What possible harm can reading do? For those who indulge in reading, we know that history has revealed the answers through men like Frederick Douglass. Knowledge is one of the greatest assets anyone can possess if understood and used properly. To attain any level of knowledge, you must be open to learning. Information abounds about virtually every topic in various written formats. For any of us to excel in our careers, spiritual life, or businesses, it is essential that we prepare ourselves adequately through reading, reading, more reading then studying, and finally, application.

The Beauty of Literature

We have the same bio-geographic roots: the people of the West Indies and Afro-America are Africans who, a few hundred years ago, were brutally uprooted from the African continent. We have shared the same past of humiliation and exploitation under slavery, and colonialism: we have also shared the glorious past of struggle, and fight against the same force. Equally important we have the same aspirations for the total liberation of all the black people in the world. Their literature, like our literature embodies all the above aspects of our struggle for a cultural identity.

—Taken from *Decolonising the Mind: The Politics of Language in African Literature* by Ngugi Wa Thiongo

"What are you doing for the long weekend?" I am going to relax and do some reading. "No, I mean what are you doing for fun?" Like I said, it will be me and the books. I have so many books in my personal library that I am dying to read, and everyday, I can find more books to add to my library. There are so many different types of books available to us. Sometimes, I read for inspiration; other times, I read strictly for pleasure, or just to remember the power of the written word. Being around books and people who enjoy books is a pleasurable experience. I have seen the impact reading has on the lives of others. Over the years, I have met several individuals who are now experts on various topics of interest. This system that we live in was created for the benefit of those who designed it. Many of my brothers don't have an institutional education and, truth be told, don't really want it; yet they are quite capable of handling the most intellectual conversation or debate. Many of us are self-educated; we have designed our own curriculum with professors we get to know through their books. Reading and education are a great source of empowerment both for individuals and for their family and their community—that is why we must take control of these aspects of our lives.

New Horizons

Reading is one of the most fundamental things that we can teach our children. It should be encouraged and required in the home each and every day. Through reading, a whole new world is opened up to our children because every aspect of life is contained in print.

—Taken from *A Black Parent's
Handbook to Educating
Your Children Outside of the
Classroom* by Baruti K. Kafele

I spent three years in college earning a diploma in business management, another two years in university earning a degree in accounting/finance, and then I entered the world looking for a good job. I never found that good job. I worked many jobs to be able to pay the bills and to make sure I was doing something more than just sitting at home feeling sorry for myself. I did take the time to examine what I learned in the education system that would help me to continue my growth in every area of my life. During my five years of post-secondary education, I became more disciplined, gained a better understanding of responsibility, learned time management, improved my communication skills, recognized the dynamics needed for successful teamwork, and became more determined to achieve my goals on my terms. Oh, let me not neglect to mention that during these five years, the works of Langston Hughes, Walter Mosley, Valerie Wesley Wilson, James Baldwin, Toni Morrison, and many many others occupied my attention right alongside my income tax act and all the other backbreaking textbooks. I was fascinated with black writers, and even with every professor warning that if you did not dedicate more hours than what exist in a day to their particular course you were doomed to failure, I still chose to spend my downtime with black books.

Building Your Library One Book at a Time:
Featuring El-Hajj Malik El-Shabazz

It is my experience that we tend to make everything a competition; we need to compare Marcus Garvey and W. E. B. DuBois, Martin Luther King Jr. and Malcolm X. It is difficult for us to examine these gentlemen as individuals with great strengths and weaknesses and who, whether they realized it or admitted it, complemented each other. The African struggle needed each one of these great men. I bought my first copy of *The Autobiography of Malcolm X* at Third World Books several years ago, and I can still remember cracking those pages open on the subway, losing myself within the pages by the time I got on the Go Bus headed for Brampton. Needless to say, I stayed up all night until my imagination brought Ossie Davis's voice alive in my head. I found Malcolm X intriguing. Reading about his transformation from criminal to black nationalist leader increased my hunger to learn more about him and others who manage to strive in the face of great adversity. Malcolm X provided me with one of several testimonies I have collected over the years about the power of reading:

> I have often reflected upon the new vistas that reading opened to me. I knew right there in prison that reading had changed forever the course of my life. As I see it today, the ability to read awoke inside me some long dormant craving to be mentally alive. I certainly wasn't seeking any degree, the way a college confers a status symbol upon its students. My homemade education gave me, with every additional book I read, a little bit more sensitivity to the deafness, dumbness, and blindness that was afflicting the black race in America. Not long ago, an English writer telephoned me from London, asking questions. One was, "What's your alma mater?" I told him, "Books." You will never catch me with a free fifteen minutes in which I'm not studying something I feel might be able to help the black man . . . I told the Englishman that my alma mater was books, a good library. Every time I catch a plane, I have with me a book that I want to read—and that's a lot of books these days. If I weren't out here every day battling the white man, I could spend the rest of my life reading, just satisfying my curiosity—because you can hardly mention anything I'm not curious about. (Taken from *The Autobiography of Malcolm X As Told to Alex Haley*)

Here is a great example of a man whose outlook and awareness about himself, his race, and his heritage completely changed once he started reading. The natural abilities that were always a part of Malcolm X started overflowing as he developed into a great orator. I challenge you to listen to this man speak—it doesn't matter whether it is a speech, lecture, or interview—then read his autobiography with an open mind to enhance learning. Those who feared Brother Malcolm's abilities killed him physically, not realizing that his spirit would continue to rise again and again.

Proud Africans

I must have said something because she said, "Fela, don't say that. Africans taught the white man. Look, the Africans have history", I said, "They don't have . . . No history man. We are slaves." She got up and brought me a book. She said I should read it". "Sandra gave me the education I wanted to know. She is the one who spoke to me about Africa. For the first time, I heard things I'd never heard before about Africa.

—Fela Anikulapo-Kuti,
speaking about Black Panther
Sandra Isadore whom he met
in New York in 1969

Why an African-centered education? We are African people! It is time for us to stop wandering the wilderness without any real direction. We don't need to get an education for the purpose of getting a good job. If education provided us with good jobs, why are so many of us still unemployed or earning incomes that barely feed our families? The need in this time is to equip ourselves with the best education to empower ourselves and our community. Our responsibility is to honor the ancestors by continuing to increase our level of consciousness to the point where we become Creators. Once we become aware of who we are and what we are capable of achieving, self-destructive behaviors will gradually fade away. There will be no need for us to wait on another man's educational system to teach our children about themselves. We will understand this is part of the process of ensuring our continuity. Take a moment to reflect on the actions of someone or any of nature's creations that are no longer in their natural element or have lost their identity. Is this what you would like for yourself, your children, or your community?

Reading with a Purpose

> I went to Washington Irving High School, at night, for a little while. And dropped out, because I could not take the time away from my job. I had gotten hold of a copy of the curriculum for required reading at the high school level, and went to second hand book stores, and bought all the books that I normally would have read in high school. I gave myself a high school education through prodigious reading, self-discipline, and self-examination.
>
> —Taken from *Dr. John Henrik Clarke: His life, His Words, His Works* by John Henrik Clarke

One of the most common myths that I encounter as a bookstore owner is that "black people don't read," which is usually funny since the person making the comment is usually not a reader himself. We are reading Bible verses, hip-hop magazines, textbooks, e-mail forwards, clothing labels, menus, European literature, and even black books. It would be insulting to my customer base for me to say that African people are not reading when my business is still growing. Of course, as a people, we do need to read more about ourselves and support authors within the African community. It is important for us to understand what we are reading and why. For those reading European writers' accounts of history, please recognize that it is still African history. We must be able to think critically when examining what appear to be facts presented to us by others whose only interest is to uplift themselves at the cost of African people. Reading can be used as a tool to open up your awareness and to satisfy one's thirst for knowledge. I encourage you to read, analytically questioning whatever you feel needs questioning while, at the same time recognizing your own personal biases that may entrap your mind. My brothers and sisters, our lives intertwine, and everything we do to improve ourselves should be extended to our community . . . read with a purpose.

Breaking Cycles

> Illusions have been created to keep us pacified, quiet and stupid about our condition. Four hundred years of systematic conditioning has created a mental condition that no longer makes plantations necessary. No longer make chains necessary. No longer makes segregation necessary. No longer requires any of those external circumstances, because the conditioning and the illusion have created such a situation so that you now operate in your own enslaving interest. We are our own primary source of enslavement.
>
> —Dr. Na'im Akbar

Imagine being whipped until your skin peeled off, being raped day after day, being tortured, and being labeled the property of another man. This is what some Africans who came before us had to endure. Five hundred years later, we have forgotten and have become complacent and lazy. We refuse to appreciate the fact that some slave master does not come and rip the baby from our arms. Today, we get the time . . . the time to prepare them to go onto the plantations willingly. It's crazy. Another people would prepare their children, train them from the womb, and open up their awareness to what lies ahead with every intention of breaking the cycle. All it takes is just a small investment. Start imparting knowledge to your child by reading and communicating once conception is known. After the child is born, continue the process and become aware of the curious nature of your baby. Your every action is being watched; and soon, you will see the determination that will make that child drag itself around, get on its knees and arms, and eventually walk. I have heard so many parents brag about the amazing things their young child is doing, yet they fail to take advantage and cautiously fill that child up with the essential knowledge it will need to navigate life. We are guides for the children who enter this physical realm without memories, making us responsible for their development.

Education

The mere imparting of information is not education. Above all things, the effort must result in making a man think and do for himself.

—Carter G. Woodson, 1933

In 1908, Carter G. Woodson attended graduate school at the University of Chicago, received his BA in March and his MA in August. In 1912, he received his PhD in history from Harvard University. In 1926, he founded Negro History Week to encourage blacks to be proud of their heritage. In his book, *The Mis-Education of the Negro*, published in 1933, he openly admits to being miseducated. This book has continued relevance today has made it a timeless classic that still graces the pages of *Essence Magazine*'s bestseller list. This Black History Month, brothers and sisters, join me in recognizing the example of Carter G. Woodson, who spent the first half of his life being miseducated and the second half reversing the process by seeking knowledge of self and creating a lasting legacy that continues to benefit the race.

Feeding the Mind

> Beyond the refusal of all exterior domination is the urge to reconnect in a deep way with Africa's cultural heritage, which has been far too long misunderstood and rejected. Far from being a superficial or folkloric attempt to bring back to life some of the traditions or practices of our ancestors, it is a matter of constructing a new African society, whose identity is not confused from outside.
>
> —Paul Zoungrana, religious
> leader from Upper Volta
> (Burkina Faso), Revolution Day
> anniversary of the 1966 coup

African men and women have made their own history, woven from the fabric of various cultures by organized actions, the development of common objectives and the manipulation of social and political symbols. This statement represents an essential truth, a must know. African people's collective need to achieve growth and development by liberating their minds is often impeded by a reluctance to identify themselves as Africans, a rejection of their natural characteristic, being unable to see beyond religious differences and constantly allowing the ego to derail efforts to unite over common goals. Brothers and sisters, self-awareness is the best medicine available to combat the previously mentioned maladies. Let us begin this process by celebrating ourselves once every week by providing our psyches with the necessary mental food.

Black Europeans

> For the Black community, the most important consequence of a white-oriented curriculum was the development of Black graduates who were useless to the Black community. A European-centered educational system produced Black Europeans who escaped from the Black community to serve as lower level flunkies in white institutions. Even worse, many Black students who wanted to use their skills to benefit the Black community found that their Euro-centric orientation made it impossible for them to communicate with Black people. Their language and values were foreign to the Black community.
>
> —Taken from *The Art of Leadership* by Oba T'Shaka

Am I a black European? All of my formal education came from a white-oriented curriculum. Even my early education in the Caribbean came from a European-centered educational system. I live in a European-dominated system. There is a good chance that I exhibit some European traits growing up here in Canada where I was expected to conform and blend in with everyone else. As a young man, I was told that I should learn to speak properly—meaning, get rid of the accent and the island dialect. Fortunately for me, I lack strong social skills and was always conscious of the reason why my parents brought me to this country—better education. I stayed focused on the education aspects and made selected friends, usually people with similar backgrounds as myself, same cultural and historical makeup, but from different islands, By the time I was in college, I knew that I wanted to go into business, whether it was working with one of my older brothers who had established businesses or developing my own. I quietly sat in on seminars and motivational talks conducted by various black groups and heard a lot of the same sentiments being expressed as I had already read in my black books. This made everything I had read and felt more real to me. The knowledge I gained outside of the educational system, along with a developing sense of self back then, helped me to maintain my identity. When it was time to choose between following a career path of becoming a professional accountant or starting my own community-based business, let's just say I followed my heart instead of the money. Don't misunderstand me, economics is important, and I have every intention of making money on my terms: doing what I enjoy and without compromising who I am. Despite my conditioning and the numerous European influences that surround me, I recognize that it is my responsibility to make sure that my African community benefits from everything that I do. I was fortunate enough to be able to provide myself with an African-centered education alongside my European-centered education, making it impossible for me to deny my community or to try and escape being an African.

Building Your Library One Book at a Time:
Featuring Amos N. Wilson

Brother Amos N. Wilson joined the ancestral realm on Saturday January 14, 1995, after creating a legacy of mind-enhancing work in the form of books. My psychology and sociology curriculum is composed of the works of the following master teachers: Dr. Amos Wilson, Dr. Na'im Akbar, Dr. Wade Nobles, Dr. Asa Hilliard, and Dr. Jacob Carruthers. One of Dr. Wilson's greatest and most in-depth contributions to the awakening of the African mind is *Blueprint for Black Power: A Moral, Political, and Economic Imperative for the Twenty-First Century*. This treasure belongs in the library of every serious African family that is committed to the long-term goal of rebuilding African people. Below is a brief excerpt from pages 129 to 130 of *Blueprint for Black Power*, dealing with the issue of African-centered education.

Afrikan's problems began with his loss of his Afrikan-centered self, his Afrikan consciousness and identity, they can only be resolved through their re-discovery, reclamation and integration into his self, consciousness and identity. There can be no substitutes. This means that the true empowerment and liberation of Afrikan peoples can only be achieved in the process of the Afrikan-education of Afrikan adults, adolescents and children in accord with Afrikan-centered curricular regimen.

Kwame Agyei Akoto impressively defines the essence and ideology of what is meant by Afrikan-centered education:

Afrikan centered education is rooted in the unique history and evolved culture of Afrikan people. It is defined in its singular commitment to the elucidation of that history, that culture, and the confirmation, invigoration and perpetuation of the Afrikan collective identity that emanates from that history and culture. Afrikan centered education is concerned with the origins, current status and the future of the Afrikan world. Afrikan centered education is committed to correcting the historical distortions born of three millennia of foreign invasion, destruction, enslavement, physical and mental colonialism, cultural disruption, and dependency. Afrikan centered education is committed to rooting or anchoring the spiritual and intellectual energies of Afrikan people in the spiritual, moral and philosophical traditions of Afrika. Afrikan centered education, whether in the several nations of the diaspora or on the motherland, is concerned to fully develop the sense of Afrikan nationality within a broader Pan Afrikan world. Afrikan centered education is concerned to sever irrevocably the pathological and slavish linkage of Afrikans to the European or Asian ethos. Afrikan centered education is concerned to enable the Afrikan person with nationbuilding, nation management, and nation maintenance abilities. Afrikan centered education is concerned to motivate teacher, student, parent and community to advance the Afrikan nation/world by any means necessary.

The future of the Afrikan world must begin with a confirmed sense of Afrikan nationality defined within the universe of Afrikan spiritual, moral and philosophical traditions and committed to the material and spiritual development and independence of the Afrikan world. Only an unambiguously Afrikan centered education can possibly accomplish this goal.

Afrikan centered education is to be distinguished from the current educational philosophies being employed in independent Afrikan nations and national enclaves in the Americas, Asia, the Pacific, and Europe. Afrikan centered education rejects the implicit and explicit superiority of European and Asian intellectual, political, and spiritual traditions that characterize the systems of former colonies, dependencies, and slave populations of the Afrikan world. It rejects the false historical notion that Asian (Arabic) and European civilization rescued Afrika from barbarism and godlessness. Afrikan centered education seeks to restore the traditions of Afrika to prominence, to revitalize those traditions and imbue them with the liberating and progressive dynamics of nationbuilding.

To Be African/Africa

Sankofa
"Go back to fetch it."
Symbol of the wisdom of learning from the past to build for the future.

Africa, the Mother of Civilization

We must never, even under the severest pressure, hate or dislike ourselves.

—Marcus Garvey

Africa and African people have been the victims of slavery, colonization, and massive propaganda that have depicted us as barbaric savages who have made no contribution to civilization. I am stating a historical fact; African people have been oppressed physically, mentally, economically, and spiritually. Mass media has done a masterful job in continuing to depict Africans as a dangerous creature that should be feared, detested, and killed. Brothers and sisters, we need to consciously strive to recognize that to hate or dislike Africa and Africans is to hate or dislike ourselves and all of humanity. It is time that we take responsibility for ourselves, and the first step is to love your African self.

Know Thyself

> The human race is of African origin. The oldest known skeletal remains of anatomically modern humans (or homo sapiens) were excavated at sites in East Africa. Human remains were discovered at Omo in Ethiopia that were dated at 195,000 years old, the oldest known in the world.
>
> —Taken from *When We Ruled*
> by Robin Walker

Africa—a continent rich in resources, history, culture, and intellectual heritage, yet there remains an impression of negativity among its children. As we enter into the month of February, celebrated as Black History Month or African Liberation Month, I am inviting you to embark upon a journey of evolution with me, intended to shatter old beliefs and replace ignorance with "knowledge." Many of the buried treasures of antiquity have been unearthed by Dr. John Henrik Clarke, John G. Jackson, Chancellor Williams, Cheikh Anta Diop, Yosef A. A. ben-Jochannan, and many many other scholars. It is now time for us to invest a little effort into getting to know ourselves. There is a time and a season for everything—"awaken the mind," "break the spell," refuse to remain in a state of slumber, and step out of the darkness into the light. No more excuses!

Ourstory

> Skeletons of pre-humans have been found in Africa that date back between 4 and 5 million years. The oldest known ancestral type of humanity is thought to have been the Australopithecus ramidus, who lived at least 4.4 million years ago.
>
> —Taken from *When We Ruled*
> by Robin Walker

The belief systems imposed upon African people have caused us to deny our homeland and withhold reverence for our ancestors whose genes we carry. Many of us still see Africa as the dark land. This pattern of thinking and the behaviors that accompany it is extremely difficult to break free off. However, with awareness and the desire for positive self-direction, we cannot only escape this mental trap but also shatter the myths that originally imprisoned us. Let's begin. Step one: Recognize "Africa is the Mother of Civilization." Many will question this statement. Good, you are ready for step two: Get up and do some research. The answers may be veiled, but they are accessible. Remember, archaeological research in Africa has been going on for some time . . . someone knows the truth . . . Is it you?

Accomplishment beyond Compare

Africans were the first to organize fishing expeditions 90,000 years ago. At Katanda, a region in northeastern Zaire (now Congo), was recovered a finely wrought series of harpoon points, all elaborately polished and barbed. Also uncovered was a tool, equally well crafted, believed to be a dagger. The discoveries suggested the existence of an early aquatic or fishing based culture.

—Taken from *When We Ruled*
by Robin Walker

Some of us are the descendants of stolen Africans, others the descendants of Africans who were explorers crossing the Atlantic long before Columbus, and still others the children who remained at home. We are all Africans with a richly endowed heritage. Our ancestors gave the world religion, as we now know it, and the beginnings of the arts, sciences, and architecture. The richness and depths of the continent called Africa has provided anthropologists, linguists, historians, and archaeologists with discoveries beyond compare. Stop minimizing anything African and anything black! Be sure to challenge your thoughts the next time you feel internal resistance when you are trying to stretch yourself to accept true knowledge about your beginning—Africa.

Equality

> Africans were the first to engage in mining 43,000 years ago. In 1964 a hematite mine was found in Swaziland at Bom vu Ridge in the Ngwenya mountain range. Ultimately 300,000 artifacts were recovered including thousands of stone-made mining tools. Adrian Boshier, one of the archaeologists on the site, dated the mine to a staggering 43,200 years old.
>
> —Taken from *When We Ruled*
> by Robin Walker

No race or ethnic group is superior to any other. Unfortunately, African people are living in a society that has willfully and systematically omitted, manipulated, and misappropriated their history. These actions were designed to bring about memory loss, to obscure vision, and to create mass confusion among Africans by impeding their critical capacities. A majority of African people have failed to do an in-depth examination of the journey starting from the beginning and progressing through each stage, describing the complete story. This failure prevents us from identifying established patterns necessary to understand what is happening to African people in this time. Brothers and sisters, our memories still remain. It is up to each of us individually to access the truth within and collectively empower ourselves beyond false issues that keep us stagnant.

365 Days of African History

Sudan has more pyramids than any other country on earth—even more than Egypt. There are at least 223 pyramids in the Sudanese cities of Al Kurru, Nuri, Gebel Barkal, and Meroe. They are generally 20 to 30 metres high and steep sided.

—Taken from *When We Ruled*
by Robin Walker

As the month of February comes to an end, life will return to normal in the schools, workplaces, and community organizations. Many will take down their posters, pack up their African history book collection, and neatly place them back in storage until next year. My understanding of the ideal objective of education is to enlighten or make students knowledgeable of the realities of their world, providing them with the understanding and skills necessary for them to improve the quality of their existence to enlighten them as to how to more effectively negotiate their survival. If this is true, why do we continue to facilitate, to a large extent, our own oppression by willingly boxing up the best examples created to inspire, transform, and propel African people to a higher spiritual level?

African People and European Consciousness

Many old West African families have private library collections that go back hundreds of years. The Mauritanian cities of Chinguetti and Oudane have a total of 3,450 handwritten mediaeval books. There may be another 6,000 books still surviving in the other city of Walata. Some date back to the 8th century AD. There are 11,000 books in private collections in Niger. Finally, in Timbuktu, Mali, there are about 700,000 surviving books.

—Taken from *When We Ruled*
by Robin Walker

Each day, I awake with the awareness that we, blacks, are Africans by virtue of our genetics and cultural ancestral heritage. Many of us find it difficult to recognize that we are conceptually incarcerated in European reality, the direct results of remaining outside of our natural environment for too long. We have been trained, educated, and indoctrinated into believing the Western concept of reality, which becomes our overall understanding of reality. The knowledge of self is crucial to the liberation of the African mind and, in turn, the African concept of reality. Consequently, we must strive toward being conscious of our own consciousness, which is essentially different from being aware of accepted realities.

Learning from the Past

Ethiopia has 11 underground mediaeval churches built by being carved out of the ground. In the twelfth and thirteenth centuries AD, Roha became the new capital of the Ethiopians. Conceived as a New Jerusalem by its founder, Emperor Lalibela (c.1150-1230), it contains 11 churches, all carved out of the rock of the mountains by hammer and chisel. All of the temples were carved to a depth of 11 metres or so below ground level. The largest is the House of the Redeemer, a staggering 33.7 metres long, 23.7 metres wide and 11.5 metres deep.

—Taken from *When We Ruled*
by Robin Walker

Even though our path is completely different from the ancestors, it is not necessary to abandon totally the old ways. We must learn to absorb the traditions of yesterday, turning them into new forms, improving upon the old, and creating more relevant traditions for today. Our ancestors somehow had the foresight to know there would come a time when we would stop being. That is precisely why we must look at our history to find the formulas or seeds to revitalize our community from the spirit. As creators, we must realize that everything that is was meant to be. In moving forward, our responsibility in rebuilding now is adequate preparation through knowledge and understanding.

Heaven on Earth

Sudan in the ninth century AD had housing complexes with bath rooms and piped water. An archaeologist wrote that Old Dongola, the capital of Makuria, had: "a[n] . . . eighth to . . . ninth century housing complex. The houses discovered here differ in their hitherto unencountered spatial layout as well as their functional programme (water supply installation, bathroom with heating system) and interiors decorated with murals."
—Taken from *When We Ruled*
by Robin Walker

Creation begins with you. My sister, my brother, you are divine. Accept this knowledge and awaken the mind to endless possibilities. But without this awareness, you will continue to struggle to know thyself. As I evolve, my understanding has shown me that all things are within me. I know that where I find myself today is a direct result of my principles, the guiding factors in the way I live my life. There was a time when the devil, environmental factors, or the next person received all the credit for my creations. Growth has blessed me with change. African people, heaven is where you stand. Open your awareness to truth, we have always been and always will be DIVINE.

Interdependent

Ibn Haukal, writing in 951 AD, informs us that the King of Ghana was "the richest king on the face of the earth" whose pre-eminence was due to the quantity of gold nuggets that had been amassed by himself and his predecessors.

—Taken from *When We Ruled*
by Robin Walker

Nobody can accomplish great things alone. We are all interconnected. That is why we need to examine why we believe that Western education has failed African people. It has not! The fact is Western education is doing an excellent job at achieving what it was designed to do. We are often confused in thinking that we are all humans and that makes our needs the same. It does not! All humans have special needs that vary according to age, sex, ethnicity, environmental differences, etc. When the specific needs of a group are not adequately met, they will be incapable of manifesting their divine talents, and that is why African parents will continue to struggle to keep their children out of special education classes.

Building Your Library One Book at a Time:
Featuring Dr. Asa Grant Hilliard III

Earlier this summer, the African community experienced yet another loss. Dr. Asa Grant Hilliard III made his transition on August 13, 2007, in Cairo, Egypt. I have long embraced the inevitability of physical death, yet each time I receive an e-mail or phone call informing me that one of our great Pan-Africans has passed on, I find myself almost in a state of panic. Dr. Hilliard III was dedicated to the rebuilding of African people as can be clearly seen in his books *SBA: The Reawakening of the African Mind* and *The Maroons within Us: Selected Essays on African American Community Socialization*. I urge you to help keep this brother alive by including his work in your library, thus keeping yourself alive. One of the first questions that always comes to mind when one of our historians passes is, "Who will continue the work?" The answer is really not that difficult; we will . . . each one of us will. Dr. Hilliard III has done his work, made his sacrifices, and left us tangible instruments for empowerment. Brothers and sisters, we just need to embrace our inheritance, give thanks to Dr. Hilliard III, and build upon his legacy. For those of you unfamiliar with Brother Hilliard's work, here is a just a small taste taken from *SBA: The Reawakening of the African Mind*:

> African people around the globe are in the midst of a MAAFA. MAAFA is a Kiswahilli term that means "disaster," (Ani, 1989). It refers to the terroristic interruption of African civilization that was occasioned by European and Arab slavery and cultural aggression. The Maafa we face is multifaceted and complete. It has produced obvious horrors like enslavement, colonization, murder, the stealing of land and property, and the systematic social, political and economic domination of Africans and African societies. It has also produced less obvious, but just as detrimental, horrors like cultural genocide, historical memory loss, and spiritual emptiness. While the MAAFA continues to rage around us, we sleep; we fail to confront our condition as a unified people because we are ignorant of our past, we have no vision for the future, and we are reactionary. In short, we do nothing as others make and execute plans for our future.

Many of us identify problems without presenting any solution; Brother Hilliard's work is balanced, it provides us with both:

To counter the MAAFA, Africans must go through a WHMY MSW, a Kemetic term which means the repetition of the birth, or a reawakening. The WHMY MSW is also a healing. But before any substantial healing can take place we Africans must "begin at the beginning" and peruse the wisdom of our ancestors. Numerous African civilizations have left the legacy of a holistic socialization process built firmly on a spiritual foundation. In these paradigmatic African societies, spirituality could not be separated from education, science, politics, health, nature, culture or anything else present in the society. This holistic approach can be useful in healing African people today.

Healing a People

> If the Blacks were among the very first builders of civilization and their
> land the birthplace of civilization, what has happened to them that
> has left them since then, at the bottom of world society, precisely what
> happened? The Caucasian answer is simple and well known: The Blacks
> have always been at the bottom. This answer is clear even in the histories
> and other educational material which whites so busily prepare for Blacks.
> Almost all of the true answers will be found in the study of the causes
> of the migrations and the tragic results stemming directly from those
> seemingly endless movements of fragmented peoples.
>
> —Taken from *The Destruction
> of Black Civilization* by
> Chancellor Williams

I will never deny the impact racism and white supremacy have had on
African people worldwide. We have suffered physically, emotionally, and
mentally! We are still suffering today. Our oppressors have remained steadfast
in their efforts in keeping us down. My people, please believe me—this is not
about anger, hatred, or blame. This is about healing! For us to move forward,
we must acknowledge truth. That is why we must stand up now and examine
our role in the destruction of African civilization. In this society, our mistakes
are often used against us to elicit specific, desired negative behaviors, making
us someone's puppet. Don't allow it! Take time to examine and understand
the ancestors' examples, good and bad. There must be no question as to who
we were and who we are—one people. Is it not time to forgive ourselves . . .
to learn to love ourselves . . . to stop the madness and start the healing?

A Divided Family

It was for reasons of security that so many of these groups, later called tribes or societies, sought the most hidden and isolated areas they could find. This permanent separation from their kinsmen in other groups was generally quite contrary to their hearts' desires. The original splintering off and parting was often done in tears. But breaking up into smaller units seemed to be the only route to survival in a permanent crisis situation—apparently permanent, since the movement of people over the continent had been going on so far beyond the memory of each generation that migrations and temporary settlements were among the most significant facts in the oral tradition of each society.

—Taken from *The Destruction
of Black Civilization* by
Chancellor Williams

If we truly understood the full extent of Africa as a continent and not as a nation, we would realize the complexity of our history. Why did disunity and mutual suspicion become an African way of life? Some of our ancestors faced the challenge of surviving the condition of lands that were often uninhabitable while trying to avoid slave hunters. In an effort to survive, they often splintered off into smaller groups that inhabited different areas. This led to a fragmentation and isolation among Africans of the same family. The consequence of all this was thousands of different dialects and languages which widened the gap between these groups. With time, each of these individual groups saw themselves as unique, their own society independent of the other and their enemies. Language and distance became instrumental in creating a divide between African people. Today, our migration continues—we still speak many different languages, have many different accents, still place distance between us, and still can't recognize our common foe.

Accepting Truth

There were, then, different outcomes for different societies. Some perished even to the last member from disease, starvation, or warfare. Others, despairing of ever again being able to have a fixed abode, became nomads. Some, although isolated so long that they had developed different languages and customs, had nevertheless decided that salvation required a union with other groups. These were the tribes that merged with other tribes, lost their separate identity and languages; and who evolved from this process a single common language, larger and larger chiefdoms, kingdoms, and finally empires that began the rebirth of their long lost civilization.

—Taken from *The Destruction of Black Civilization* by Chancellor Williams

For deep truth, our study of our African past must be in-depth, balanced, and lifelong. We must question, seek answers, question some more, and then sit in silence and listen. The very nature of life is change; and every time we awaken our mind to truth, increasing our level of consciousness, transformation is taking place. As a child, I saw my people as uncivilized savages indulging in cannibalism and barbarism. As I reflect on those days, it disturbs me to realize and admit that my mind was a dumping ground for others. Yet it gives me great joy to know that subconsciously, Truth was always a part of me. Somehow, I knew there was more, and it is slowly being revealed with my growth. Today, I am not afraid to say yes—some of my ancestors surrendered to a fate of indifference, others grew too weak to continue to fight, and still others descended to their lowest level of being. This too is a part of our story that must be understood in the context of the time and the situation . . . survival.

Forgetting Our Customs

Your attention is called again to the map of Africa, for it is very significant where the earliest invaders entered and permanently settled. They took over the areas of trade that allowed easy contact with their homeland and the other nations of the world. This is a point that simply cannot be overstressed in considering the plight of the African people. In the north they settled around the Mediterranean, thereby maintaining contact with Europe and Asia. In the northeast, east, and south, they settled along the Red Sea and the Indian Ocean, thereby keeping in touch with their homeland and the trade countries farther away. Black Africa was thus hemmed in and effectively cut off, commercially and otherwise, from the rest of the world.

—Taken from *The Destruction
of Black Civilization* by
Chancellor Williams

Imagine an all-African army under Asian officers moving against fellow Africans. How could this be? It was once a universal practice to enslave the captives of war. African chiefs and kings took it a step further and sold those slaves to the Arabs. Once the trade in prisoners of war became a primary source of wealth for these leaders, traditional customs were no longer observed. A strong sense of community and brotherhood became less predominant in African life. This set in motion a chain of events that would weaken some of the most advanced societies in Africa. The continent of Africa and black Africans have always had what the world wanted: gold, diamonds, ivory, copper, iron ore, and themselves. Once the invaders or Arabs realized the weakening bonds among Africans, they started inland raids for slaves. There were many chiefs and kings that resisted these attacks; however, the process of creating our greatest enemy had begun.

Religious Invaders

> Other invaders found penetration easy under the banners of religion. Full advantage was taken of the fact that Africans are a very religious people. First came the Crescent flag of the Prophet. The Islamic advance was three-pronged: proselytizing missions claiming one brotherhood; widespread intermarriages and concubinage with African women, due to the Muslim system of polygamy; and forceful conversions at sword point. The Cross of Jesus Christ followed the Muslim Crescent. The cloak of Christianity was a most convenient hiding place for those who had other designs. Hence, the drive to convert. Conversion here meant far more than conversion to Christianity. As in the case of Islam, it meant change into the white man's image, his ideas and value system.
>
> —Taken from *The Destruction of Black Civilization* by Chancellor Williams

There can be no doubt that to understand Africa thoroughly, we must examine the effects of Islam and Christianity upon the continent and its indigenous spiritual practices. Both the Arabs and the Europeans came in search of resources and captured Africans for the purpose of slave labor. Invaders, conquerors, oppressors, and dominant powers have always and will always force their religious belief system and culture upon those being oppressed. Africans who did not convert to Islam or Christianity were labeled as savage pagans. Many of those Africans who became Muslims and Christians no longer considered themselves African, quickly adopting Arabic and Christian names. The African family experienced more division brought about by new foreign religious practices that encouraged self-hate. Africans everywhere today are still psychologically shackled by manipulative religious practices that have been designed to keep us from loving our sisters, our brothers, and ourselves.

To Live or Die: A People's Choice

Egypt, as pointed out before, was the North-Eastern region of ancient Ethiopia. The six cataracts of the Nile were the great watermarks in the heartland of the Blacks from whence African culture spread over the continent, but nowhere was it pronounced as in Egypt. This northern sector of Ethiopian empire had been the object of world attention from the earliest times. The fact was that it was in the center of the crossroads from all directions leading into Africa from Asia and Europe. This also explains how the Asians came to occupy and control a fourth of Egypt (Lower Egypt) before the unification of the "Two Lands" in the third millennium B.C.

—Taken from *The Destruction of Black Civilization* by Chancellor Williams

4000 BC onward saw Africans in the Asian-held areas in the north making more difficult choices. All throughout the continent, Africans were faced with remaining in their home region with the possibility of being reduced to the status of servant or slave; or if they were from the higher professional class of that region, they could remain and integrate with the Asians and, in many instances, assume high-ranking positions; or they could refuse to integrate with Asian society in any form and migrate southward. The majority of Africans fled the area. There were also many Africans who refused to flee the area and never submitted to slavery. They perished! The Africans held Upper Egypt (South), and the Asians held Lower Egypt (North). Once the Asians and their children (from African women) gained control, the Africans' decline to the bottom of the social, economic, and political ladder became inevitable.

Self-love or Racism

I only want to reclaim myself / I even want you / to reclaim yourself.
—Nikki Giovanni

I am often accused of being a racist! Why? At age twenty-one, I made a conscious choice for growth and self-development, learning to identify and accept the negative and positive aspects of my personality. My journey of self-help, self-discovery, and self-preservation took root. Learning to listen to my inner voice awakened my mind to the importance of re-examining my conditioning from birth. During this process, I discovered some serious problems with my education, family, religious beliefs, economic practices, and psychology. Today, my knowledge of self will no longer allow me to live my life based on another man's truth that ignores my very existence. Now, brothers and sisters, if the fact that I pray to my African God, love my African self, and love my African people makes me a racist . . .

Building Your Library One Book at a Time:
Featuring Marcus Garvey

Marcus Garvey journeyed to the United States in an effort to meet Booker T. Washington, the founder of Tuskegee. After reading Booker T. Washington's book *Up from Slavery*, Garvey was inspired. Unfortunately, by the time he actually made it to the United States, Washington had died. Marcus Garvey went on to build a mass movement among African Americans, advocating the return of Africa to the Africans and people of African descent. This brother was a fireball, a great orator, and one of the greatest Pan-Africans ever. Although Marcus Garvey was in a federal prison by 1926, his movement in the five years previous had a fantastic life span. Many would argue that Marcus Garvey failed. I know that he did not, for I am benefiting from his great legacy at this very moment. Marcus had a genuine love for African people and Africa. If you don't know anything about this great African, I would recommend reading *The Philosophy and Opinions of Marcus Garvey*, *Message to the People*, and *Race First*. Here is an opportunity for a little taste of Garvey's passionate attempts at inspiring a once-great race back to its greatness:

> To read the histories of the world, peoples and races, written by white men, would make the Negro feel and believe that he never amounted to anything in creation. History is written with prejudices, likes and dislikes; and there has never been a white historian who ever wrote with any true love or feeling for the Negro.

> The Negro should expect but very little by way of compliment from the pen of other races. We are satisfied to know, however, that our race gave the first great civilization to the world; and, for centuries Africa, our ancestral home, was the great seat of learning; and when black men, who were only fit then for the company of the gods, were philosophers, artists, scientists and men of vision and leadership, the people of other races were groping in savagery, darkness and continental barbarism.

> White historians and writers have tried to rob the black man of his proud past in history, and when anything new is discovered to support the race's claim and attest the truthfulness of our greatness in other ages, then it is skillfully rearranged and credited to some other unknown race or people.

Negroes, teach your children that they are direct descendants of the greatest and proudest race who ever peopled the earth; and it is because of the fear of our return to power, in a civilization of our own, that may outshine others, why we are hated and kept down by a jealous and prejudiced contemporary world.

The very fact that the other races will not give the Negro a fair chance is indisputable evidence and proof positive that they are afraid of our civilized progression. Every falsehood that is told by the historian should be unearthed, and the Negro should not fail to take credit for the glorious and wonderful achievements of his fathers in Africa, Europe and Asia.

Black men were so powerful in the earlier days of history that they were able to impress their civilizations, culture and racial characteristics and features upon the people of Asia and Southern Europe. The dark Spaniards, Italians and Asiatics are the colored offspring of a powerful black African civilization and nationalism. Any other statement by historians to the contrary is "bunk" and should not be swallowed by the enlightened Negro.

When we speak of 400,000,000 Negroes we mean to include several of the millions of India who are direct offspring of that ancient African stock that once invaded Asia. The 400,000,000 Negroes of the world have a beautiful history of their own, and no one of any other race can truly write it but themselves. Until it is completely and carefully written, for the guidance of our children and ourselves, let us think it.

The white man's history is his inspiration, and he would be untrue to himself and negligent of the rights of his posterity to subordinate it to others, and so also of the Negro. Our history is as good as that of any other race of people, and nothing on this side of Heaven or Hell will make us deny it, the false treaties, essays, speculations, and philosophies of others notwithstanding. (Taken from "History and the Negro" from *The Philosophy and Opinions of Marcus Garvey*)

Nation Building

Nkonsonkonson
   "A chain, or a link."
   Symbol of unity, responsibility, interdependence, brotherhood, and cooperation.

Self-Reliance

No man will do as much for you as you will do for yourself.
—Marcus Garvey

We must remain steadfast in our efforts to build a better and richer life for us as a people. Brothers and sisters, a conscious decision to love oneself and one's community will help the flames of liberation to burn much brighter with each day. Let us not forget, it is the power of "Black Love" that created Marcus Garvey, Nat Turner, Assata Shakur, and Harriet Tubman. It is that same power we must embrace today with the purpose of rescuing each other, our culture, and our history.

The Future of the Race

> Our children may learn about heroes of the past. Our task is to make ourselves architects of the future.
>
> —Jomo Kenyatta

As grandparents, parents, aunts, uncles, brothers, sisters, cousins, and godparents, we are all members of the village; and we have a duty to prepare our children today for tomorrow. The survival and progress of African people will depend on our collective commitment to building strong infrastructures. Brothers and sisters, let us not ignore the fact that each of us have a role to play and a contribution to make in this process. It's time to take the first step . . . question thyself . . . get to know thyself . . . accept responsibility for thyself . . . recognize that we are creating the blueprint for the future of African people in the children of today.

It Takes a Village

If we lose (our) love and self-respect and respect for each other, this is how we will finally die.

—Maya Angelou

On this day, I will use my love as a source of strength and support for my community. We are in great need of healing from the hurt and pain of hopelessness, despair, and anger. We are afraid of each other; a simple greeting of acknowledgement will incite fear in us. We no longer embrace the great African proverb "It takes a village to raise a child"; and, brothers, we are no longer prepared to be our brother's keeper. Creator has charged us each with the responsibility of contributing to the betterment of humanity through the use of our individual talents. Our challenge is to prepare the foundation for honest dialogue and exchange, to be able to sit at the table and commune with each other even when we disagree. It is imperative that we edify one another with our individual gifts and use these gifts for the building of our community. Come on, brothers and sisters, let us work together!

Appreciating Mothers

> Next to God we are indebted to women, first for life itself, and then for making it worth living.
>
> —Mary Mcleod Bethune

Now, this is the chronology of life. A seed is planted. Life emerges from the womb of woman. Love is brought forth in the form of a mother. We awake to gentle hands and knowing heart with the insight to provide little beings with nurturing care. Mother! And through the changing seasons of life, mother's love remains a delightful gift from the Creator. She is our fortress in times of trouble, our sanctuary from despair, and our haven where love abounds. Those of us with sight will return mother's love, knowing that darkness will once again beckon her into the light of a new journey. On this day, I give thanks to the Creator for the blessings bestowed upon me through the ones called grandmother, mother, aunt, sister, wife, daughter . . . woman.

A Father's Example

> Your face reflected a most peaceful state. I felt your final breath as your
> spirit ascended to another place.
>
> —Sean Liburd

In my moments of quiet contemplation, my heart is nourished as I travel the road called remembrance. For me, it is a pleasant walk filled with joy and sorrow, leading to a place of appreciation. At birth, I was blessed with one who would continue to build upon the foundation of the ancestors. He served decisively, accepting his responsibility as a provider, nurturer, protector, and authority figure. Today, I give thanks for the male spirit that functioned as my guide for thirty years, demonstrating love of family, community building, self-determination, and the courage to grow beyond self. Brothers and sisters, my father was imperfect; however, he was the example I needed. The rest is up to me.

Investing in the Children

Help your children develop a passion in life . . . . They need an abiding interest to occupy their minds and keep them from the many devastating temptations of our society.

—Myrlie Evers-Williams

We frequently speak about the children being the future and how we need to provide them with direction and inspiration. It's true. Our treatment and investment in the children will determine the future of this world. It is therefore our responsibility to prepare children at a young age by offering them the love, respect, and guidance needed. We must awaken their minds with knowledge beyond academics. The focus must be on the children, making them the center of attention. The communal family must serve as a model for the children to emulate. Brothers and sisters, this summer, let's expose, educate, and appreciate our children and ourselves.

Controlling Your Money

> While many believe that only the wealthy have economic power, all of
> us have the power to spend our money where we choose, whether we're
> making a million-dollar purchase or buying a box of detergent.
>
> —Camille Cosby

Money can be spent, invested, or kept idle. Over the past few years, we have been bombarded with numerous statistics showing how much money the African/black community contributes to the economy annually. It is apparent that we have money and, more importantly, we love to spend it. Brothers and sisters, we are one of the richest people on this planet. We are blessed with great spiritual strength, and the dollar we each hold in the palm of our hand will easily multiply at the moment we realize one hand can't clap. The choice is ours . . .

Serving

> I am because we are; and since we are, therefore I am.
>
> —John S. Mbiti

One of the greatest blessings of my life has been Knowledge Bookstore. Over the past ten years, my work has provided me with a vast array of experiences within my community. Today, I give thanks for all of the support, encouragement, and love provided to me. I am deeply grateful for the opportunity to be of service to my brothers and sisters. Each of us has a contribution to make, and I am aware of many who are making a difference simply by doing their part. So let us not allow ourselves to be overcome by negativity while fulfilling the will of Creator. We are each other's fate!

Teamwork

Many Eyes One Vision.

—African Image Makers

Individuals with different personal visions often get together as a team with a shared vision. This collective vision will ultimately determine the direction of the team. Teamwork provides a unique opportunity to turn vision into reality. However, more often than not, there will be conflicts around the vision. These conflicting ideas can enhance the creative process and discover new solutions to help advance the team. Brothers and sisters, as a community, we are a team that must learn to take the vision from ME to WE.

Partnership

> We are each other's harvest: we are each other's business: we are each
> other's magnitude and bond.
>
> —Gwendolyn Brooks in
> "Paul Robeson"

We know that as a people, solidarity is essential to our rebirth, making it time to create an awareness that will help to gradually remove chaos from our presence. That is why cultivating an understanding of our shared values and goals is imperative to building trust, the prerequisite to cooperation among us. We must integrate ourselves back together again. Today, I am pleased to highlight the Grand African Market Place, a partnership between Knowledge Bookstore and MACPRI (Mother Africa's Children Photographic Reproductions International). The seven principles of the Nguzo Saba—unity, self-determination, collective work and responsibility, cooperative economics, purpose, creativity, and faith—are at the foundation of this relationship. Two African businesses dedicated to the liberation of all Africans. May the ancestors be pleased!

Giving Back

The greatest thing a person can do is contribute to the well-being of another.

—Jim Brown

Relax your body: your buttocks, shoulders, stomach, back of your head, neck, cheeks, and jaw muscles. Take a deep breath in through the nose and release it back out of the nose. Clear your mind of all thoughts. Feel your thoughts, tensions, and worries leaving your body and returning to space. Keep breathing in and out. Follow the stream of words before you like sounds that resound in your head, and listen to their echo. All praise and thanks to Creator for his infinite wisdom and guidance throughout this journey. Respect the ancestors who served as an example. And to my brothers and sisters that I walk among, please accept my humble offering of appreciation for all of your love and support.

Upliftment

> If you have no confidence in self, you are twice defeated in the race of life.
>
> —Marcus Garvey

Knowledge Bookstore is a celebration of the wondrous achievements of Africans and their descendants worldwide. At Knowledge, our goal is a journey of "self-knowledge" for the purpose of uplifting the consciousness of the African (black) community. It is our hope to inform people of African origin that they have a priceless and proud heritage that they need to acknowledge, support, and cultivate. The Knowledge family is committed to providing the tools to promote racial and cultural pride and is dedicated to learning, sharing, and teaching the true history of Africans worldwide. It is our intention to reintroduce the contributions and significance of Africa to the world. Creators, it is time to "awaken the mind."

Why a Pan-African Museum and Library?

We must learn to tell our own story and to tell our own history.
—John Henrik Clarke

Pan-Africanism is a movement of solidarity among Africans to recover or reclaim history, culture, or national pride. It is the embodiment of Peter Tosh's lyrics, "As long as you are a black man, you are an African." Africans worldwide have shared a common history struggling against racism, white supremacy, slavery, colonialist exploitation, neocolonialism, and imperialism. The Pan-African movement is committed to returning the full dignity to African (black) people by challenging and erasing the lies and distortions that have been propagated by European and American literature. The Pan-Africanist is charged with the duty of preserving ancient African history, documenting present-day history, and ensuring the full participation of African people in the political, cultural, social, and economic dimensions of world affairs.

Knowledge Bookstore and Sankofaincipher is pleased to show reverence to great African men and women who have demonstrated the ideals of Pan-Africanism with the launching of the Pan-African Museum and Library. It is our hope that the spirit of these Africans, past and present, will be a source of inspiration that will continue to mobilize African people, no matter where they are found on the face of this earth today, toward unification.

Giving Thanks

In my music, my plays, my films, I want to carry always this central idea: to be African. Multitudes of men have died for less worthy ideals: it is even more eminently worth living for.

—Paul Robeson

On behalf of Knowledge Bookstore and Sankofaincipher, I would like to express our appreciation to everyone that came out to support the launch of the Pan-African Museum and Library. I would also like to acknowledge the following individuals for their contributions to the building process: Andrew Martin, Brother Oji, Francis McLean, Karen McLean, Kevin Jones, Neil Armstrong, Sankofa, Derek Williams, Michele Liburd, Carolette Liburd, Sensa Ra Neb, Ramanau, Noreen Etto, and D'we. An extra special thanks to the African men and women who are featured in the Pan-African Museum for being the example of living a life with a sense of purpose beyond self.

Building Your Library One Book at a Time:
Featuring Dr. Frances Cress Welsing

Can black people save themselves? Each new generation should present a new opportunity for us as a people to reconnect to our true nature. The life we live is greater than each of us is individually. Our time here physically will eventually expire, that is why the children must be prepared to continue to build onto the work of the previous generation. Dr. Frances Cress Welsing, a psychiatrist, has produced a thought-provoking collection of essays examining the white supremacy, the symbolism in today's society, the black child, and the process of inferiority, plus the crises in black male-female relationships. *The Isis Papers* confronts the global system of white supremacy that has been used to oppress nonwhites worldwide. This brilliant sister shows no fear in challenging a power system of racism and those who uphold it. Her work is thought provoking and may even be considered controversial to many. Dr. Cress Welsing states clearly her thoughts on a very important issue:

> Black children are our most valuable possession and our greatest potential resource. Any meaningful discussion of the survival or the future of Black people must be predicated upon Black people's plan for the maximal development of all Black children. Children are the only future of any people. If the children's lives are squandered, and if the children of a people are not fully developed at whatever cost and sacrifice, the people will have consigned themselves to certain death. They will be destroyed from without or from within—by the attack of their own children against them. And they may be destroyed by both. Black people now are being attacked in the streets (from within) by our own youths, as well as being attacked (from without) by a collective oppressor. This reality reveals the central questions of this essay, which Black people must answer: 1) Will Black children in the U.S. ever develop to their maximum genetic potential? 2) If so, who will assume ultimate responsibility for bringing about that maximal development—Black people themselves or white people? 3) If Black children are not to be maximally developed, what do Black people really think is going to happen to this large Black undeveloped mass of human beings? And, 4) Are white people in any way looking to Black people for the maximal development of white children?

The Power of Thoughts

Dwennimmεn
"Ram's Horns."
Symbol of strength (in mind, body, and soul), humility, wisdom, and learning.

State of Mind

It takes a revolution to find a solution.

—Bob Marley

It is time to break out of our prisons of private pain. Suffering is a universal language. We all know what it is to be overwhelmed by obstacles causing our resolve to weaken and allowing pain to take residence within our hearts. It hurts to watch your dreams fade away, to watch fear and worries cloud your perspective. Stop! Remember! Never lose sight of the fact that life is a journey of varied experiences all necessary to our growth. Brothers and sisters, the revolution begins with your state of mind. It is completely in our control to slowly practice planting seeds of right thoughts that will evolve into our tomorrow, provided we remain patient and persistent. This we must never forget.

Living in the Moment

> Even the smallest victory is never to be taken for granted. Each victory must be applauded, because it is so easy not to battle at all, to just accept and call that acceptance inevitable.
>
> —Audre Lord

Life is painfully difficult. We constantly face self-doubt, frustration, anger, blame, and victimization in dealing with life's problems. It is amazing how the fear of failure coupled with negative thoughts can cripple our ability to see beyond the obstacles. Still, many of us are waiting for a better tomorrow, not realizing that today IS tomorrow. Brothers and sisters, today's victory matters and should be acknowledged and celebrated. We must always remember to give thanks to the Creator for the divine gift of life itself. As for myself, this moment is a celebration!

Learning Our Lessons

Mistakes are a fact of life. It is the response to the error that counts.
—Nikki Giovanni

Everybody makes mistakes, strays, and fails. What does this mean? As humans, we will learn lessons. Life lessons are repeated until they are learned. If they are not learned the easy way, then they will get more difficult. When the lesson is learned, we will correct our actions and then move on. Brothers and sisters, failure is never final, it is a guide to the path that each of us must travel. If we are to attain a higher level of being, it is imperative that we embrace the process of repeated failures and constant struggle. These experiences will provide us with the ability to make adjustments in our lives, making it easier to fail forward.

Building upon the Foundation

> We will not sprint to victory. Rather, we are long-distance runners in a relay race. We have come too far to be side-tracked or detoured or to get weak in the knees and not go the distance.
>
> —Susan L. Taylor

Patience is a difficult quality to develop in a fast-paced society. Yet it is an essential trait that needs to be cultivated if we plan to go the distance. It is inevitable that, at some point in time, doubts will become a companion on the journey. They cloud our vision and make it difficult to see the ultimate goal. These are the times we will question our purpose and give in to hopelessness, thinking those things will never change and that it's all just a waste of time. When I find myself in this situation, I try my best to change focus, stop the pity party, and remember, brothers and sisters, that our role is not to finish the work that was begun. Our responsibility is to continue building upon the strong foundation laid by our ancestors while preparing our children for the next leg of the race.

We Are a Reflection of Our Daily Practice

> It's important to stay committed and keep doing your job well, but use free time to pursue your dream . . . . You'll know when it's time to leave.
>
> —Terrie Williams

One of the most common excuses for slacking off at work is, "I hate this job." In our misery, we fail to hold ourselves to a high standard of performance. Thus, our mental attitude becomes poor, limiting us to a prison of our own creation. It is important for us to realize that when we practice negative work ethics, these characteristics remain a part of us. Consequently, when we decide to pursue our own dreams, we are faced with the unpleasant undertaking of overcoming a self-imposed barrier originally devised to hurt someone else. Brothers and sisters, we must give up the delusion that our lack of efficiency and effectiveness on the job will not hurt us over the long run.

Acknowledging Spirit

Take a moment to acknowledge and celebrate life's journey.

—Sean Liburd

Life has and will always provide its challenges. It is a journey designed to allow us to experience the universal balance of right and wrong mental conditions, which will result in positive or disastrous effects upon one's life. I am not where I would like to be yet. I give thanks to Creator for providing me with several opportunities to face defeat and celebrate triumph. It is good for us to take a moment to recognize the works being done through our spirit. Now is the time to honor yourself for being able to show compassion to others, giving birth, nurturing a family, building a community, forgiving yourself, not giving up, and being able to give and embrace love . . . .

Thoughts Determine Feelings

> Our elevation must be the result of self-efforts, and work of our own
> hands. No other human power can accomplish it. If we but determine
> it shall be so, it will be so.
>
> —Martin R. Delany, 1852

Have you ever realized how closely associated thoughts and feelings are?
For example, if you think that your community is becoming really dangerous
for yourself and your family, your feelings toward it will change. You will no
longer want to remain a part of it. On the other hand, if you discover living
in another community that you have never felt any special affection for can be
beneficial. You will begin to love that community. Our feelings vary according
to our thoughts, and once feelings are involved, they spur us to act. Let us
be aware that thought is power, and when combined with feeling and desire,
some kind of action will follow.

Understanding

> If you wish to be a master you must love impersonally, caring for all equally; wants must yield to self control, live as though you have achieved and acquired everything you need and also as if you have lost everything; even the thing or person you might love most; for material things are transitory.
>
> —Taken from *Egyptian Proverbs* by Dr. Muata Ashby

If each of us could see the world as an expression of his or her heart, our innermost self, we would delight in the beauty that is our existence. Our basic nature is to engage in thought that will eventually manifest itself into action creating our external reality, the world. We are all endowed with Creator's greatest gift: love. Yet we lack understanding of the Divine presence within. Our happiness is often based upon something outside of ourselves such as others, activities, and possessions. This is a place of ignorance that most of us will travel to. Some will choose to make a bed in this place, while others will come into recognition that this place is nothing more than a thought.

Media Influences

> Tell me who's got control of your mind, your worldview. Is it the news
> or the movie you taking your girl to?
>
> —Dead Prez

Television, film, radio, books, and the World Wide Web are powerful forces that saturate the mind and body with sights and sounds that influence psychological, emotional, and spiritual well-being. Once we are mindful of this fact, the challenge to balance out our viewing, reading, and listening habits with sounds, words, and images which soothe our souls and add to our collective worth becomes our responsibility. Modern media has been one of the greatest tools used to create negative influence against African people. Brothers and sisters, there is no need for us to be outraged by the media. Instead, let us insulate ourselves and our families as best as we can from these negative effects.

Anger

> For the only love that exists is the love we make.
>
> —Prince

Many of us exist in a place surrounded by heavy clouds and lingering entities of darkness that are patiently awaiting their opportunity to go out into space doing untold damage. Be guarded against anger, for when it breaks out, it blinds the angry one from everything. When we are consumed in the ugliness of anger, our natural disposition of beauty quickly fades away. In that moment of burning anger, we cannot see the ugliness that becomes us. It is only seen when demonstrated by another. We must all be careful not to become the creator of innumerous damage caused by our negative thoughts and feelings projected into the universe. "Be watchful, my brother, my sister!" Let us not be a victim of uncontrollable emotions.

Escaping Negative Emotions

You've got to get the mind cleaned out before you can put the truth in it.
—Minister Louis Farrakhan

At this very moment, someone is being betrayed. Someone else is mistreated while another heart is being broken as a result of negative actions. At some point in time, we have all been impacted by the actions of another, or our actions have created difficulties for others. These experiences often become a guiding force in our lives without our awareness. We become vengeful, angry, ashamed, or guilt ridden. The truth is clouded with our belief about right and wrong, good and bad. We forget that none of us is without faults, nor will any of us go through life without being the gateway for another's pain. We beat up ourselves for falling short of expectations and use a lot of energy, assigning blame to oneself or others, for our state of mind or emotional malady. If we could just manage to create a shift of energy in our mind, we will gradually begin to realize that healing is necessary.

Building Your Library One Book at a Time:
Featuring Martin Luther King Jr.

One of the greatest and most admired speeches of our time is "I have a dream" by Martin Luther King Jr. This speech is part of the great legacy Dr. King left behind for the world. I have heard many criticisms of Dr. King and have also had a few of my own, but I would never deny that Brother Martin was one of our greatest examples. I have grown to recognize it takes something very special to be able to keep turning the other cheek while another man kicks you, hits you, spits on you, throws you in jail, sets his dogs on you, and just keeps abusing you physically and mentally. Dr. King not only endured all of this, he never ran away. He kept hope alive within himself and thousands of others to keep going back to the battlefield. He demonstrated true courage. Many of us would resort to fighting violence with violence, and that may be our role to play. Martin Luther King Jr. understood the power of words and worked with his ability not only to string words together in a most profound way but also to deliver them to the core of a human being. Dr. King was fighting for African people in America with a universal message that provided inspiration for oppressed people everywhere. His messages were twofold. On one hand, he was trying to keep hope alive for African people being treated worst than animals, and he was also saying to Europeans in America to stop acting like savages. He knew Europeans had lost their humanity traveling all over the world, leaving destruction and chaos behind. He also knew it was time to make a stand and to send the message that this type of treatment is no longer acceptable. Brothers and sisters, before we judge Dr. Martin Luther King Jr. as a weak man, a sellout, or place any other negative connotation next to his name, we should read his words carefully:

We cannot walk alone. And as we walk, we must make the pledge that we shall march ahead. We cannot turn back. There are those who are asking the devotees of civil rights, "When will you be satisfied?" we can never be satisfied as long as our bodies, heavy with the fatigue of travel, cannot gain lodging in the motels of the highways and the hotels of the cities. We cannot be satisfied as long as the Negro's basic mobility is from a smaller ghetto to a larger one. We can never be satisfied as long as a Negro in Mississippi cannot vote and a Negro in New York believes he has nothing for which to vote. No, no, we are not satisfied, and we will not be satisfied until justice rolls down like waters and righteousness like a mighty stream.

Go back to Mississippi, go back to Alabama, go back to Georgia, go back to Louisiana, go back to the slums and ghettos of our northern cities, knowing that somehow this situation can and will be changed. Let us not wallow in the valley of despair. I say to you today, my friends, that in spite of the difficulties and frustrations of the moment, I still have a dream. It is a dream deeply rooted in the American dream.

I have a dream that one day this nation will rise up and live out the true meaning of its creed: "We hold these truths to be self-evident: that all men are created equal." I have a dream that one day on the red hills of Georgia the sons of former slaves and the sons of former slaveowners will be able to sit down together at a table of brotherhood. I have a dream that one day even the state of Mississippi, a desert state, sweltering with the heat of injustice and oppression, will be transformed into an oasis of freedom and justice. I have a dream that my four children will one day live in a nation where they will not be judged by the color of their skin but by the content of their character. I have a dream today.

I have a dream that one day the state of Alabama, whose governor's lips are presently dripping with the words of interposition and nullification, will be transformed into a situation where little black boys and black girls will be able to join hands with little white boys and white girls and walk together as sisters and brothers. I have a dream today. I have a dream that one day every valley shall be exalted, every hill and mountain shall be made low, the rough places will be made plain, and the crooked places will be made straight, and the glory of the Lord shall be revealed, and all flesh shall see it together. This is our hope. This is the faith with which I return to the South. With this faith we will be able to hew out of the mountain of despair a stone of hope. With this faith we will be able to transform the jangling discords of our nation into a beautiful symphony of brotherhood. With this faith we will be able to work together, to pray together, to struggle together, to go to jail together, to stand up for freedom together, knowing that we will be free one day.

This will be the day when all of God's children will be able to sing with a new meaning, "My country, 'tis of thee, sweet land of liberty, of thee I sing. Land where my fathers died, land of the pilgrim's pride, from every mountainside, let freedom ring." And if America is to be a great nation, this must become true. So let freedom ring from the prodigious hilltops of New Hampshire. Let freedom ring from the mighty mountains of New York. Let freedom ring from the heightening Alleghenies of Pennsylvania! Let freedom ring from the snowcapped Rockies of Colorado! Let freedom ring from the curvaceous peaks of California! But not only that; let freedom ring from Stone Mountain of Georgia! Let freedom ring from Lookout Mountain of Tennessee! Let freedom ring from every hill and every molehill of Mississippi. From every mountainside, let freedom ring.

When we let freedom ring, when we let it ring from every village and every hamlet, from every state and every city, we will be able to speed up that day when all of God's children, black men and white men, Jews and Gentiles, Protestants and Catholics, will be able to join hands and sing in the words of the old Negro spiritual, "Free at last! free at last! Thank God Almighty, we are free at last!" ("I have a dream" by Martin Luther King Jr., April 23, 1963, at Lincoln Memorial, Washington, D.C.)

You have read a portion of the "I have a dream" speech, now make it your mission to get the speech in its entirety. Read it again, study his words, then listen to his words, and then study his actions. It's not over yet, the journey has just begun. Seek out the "Beyond Vietnam" speech and "I've been to the mountaintop" speech and go through the process again. *A Call to Conscience: The Landmark Speeches of Dr. Martin Luther King, Jr.* is an excellent source to help become better acquainted with the words of Dr. King. Brother Martin shared with us a dream that was much greater than himself, one he knew he would not live to see. How many of us have dreams like that today?

Honoring the Ancestors

Baobab
   "Found in northeastern, central, and southern Africa."
   Some are said to be thousands of years old.

History

> The events which transpired 5,000 years; five years ago or five minutes ago, have determined what will happen five minutes from now; five years from now or 5,000 years from now. All history is a current event.
>
> —Dr. John Henrik Clarke

Dr. John Henrik Clarke was eighty-three years old when he made his transition on July 16, 1998. He was a college professor, internationally respected historian, book reviewer, curriculum specialist, writer, poet, captivating lecturer, and considered by most the Father of Black Studies. On behalf of Knowledge Bookstore, I would like to recognize Dr. John Henrik Clarke as a great Pan-Africanist and one of our greatest historians. Brothers and sisters, let us honor him by showing appreciation for his years of service re-educating us about African history. Dr. John Henrik Clarke has done his part, providing us with a compass; now it is up to us to use it to regain our spiritual, economical, political, and cultural direction.

Remembering through Celebrations

When you kill the ancestor, you kill yourself.

—Toni Morrison

The long weekend is over. Caribana in Toronto is done. Antigua's Carnival will end today. Crop Over in Barbados will wrap up on Wednesday. Nevis's Culturama cools down on Wednesday. Each of these festivals features traditions and various aspects of our culture such as music and dance. All of these celebrations originated from the abolition of slavery in the Caribbean. August Monday, also known as Emancipation Day, is a day for us as a community to remember the ancestors who fought for the freedoms we all enjoy today. Brothers and sisters, it is my hope that if you were unable to give the ancestors a moment yesterday, you will dedicate a moment today and give thanks.

The Warrior's Path

> The struggle is far from over. There is much more to be said and much more to be done.
>
> —Harry Belafonte

There is so much work that has already been done by the ancestors, yet there is still a great deal of work to be done by us in this time. More than ever, we need to remember the spirit of African warriors and the great examples they left for us. In order to do all things society dictates, we are conditioned to sleepwalk our way through life, ignoring the voice of Creator who constantly calls to us for an awakening. Brothers and sisters, take a moment to think about the people you respect and admire. What is it that they possess that you don't, and please go a little bit deeper than the surface, for money is not an acceptable answer. The time has long passed for an explosion of consciousness to come over African people.

White Jesus No More

My main point here is that if you are the child of God and God is a part of you, then in your imagination God suppose to look like you. And when you accept a picture of the deity assigned to you by another people, you become the spiritual prisoners of that other people.

—John Henrik Clarke

White Jesus! White angels! Damn! A few days ago, this nun came into my place of business trying to sell me some calendars, raising funds for a cause that I cannot recall. I have grown accustomed to strangers walking in off the street looking for donations for one cause or another, children selling chocolates for their schools, or sporting team and others calling on the phone, trying to get a few dollars for their organizations. Charitable giving is an essential part of my spiritual life. Growing up with a mother who was always giving to others, and still gives, makes it easy for me to give without expecting anything in return. I am involved in projects specifically developed for the purpose of helping my brothers and sisters here in Canada, in the Caribbean, and in Africa. I have more than enough worthy causes to donate to, still I will buy that chocolate bar to encourage a young child, pledge $20 for ride for heart, or give a couple of dollars just for asking. White Jesus! White angels! Hell, no! I looked around at my sanctuary, my business, and then looked that nun in the eyes and simply said, "No thanks, that's not going to work here." I am not sure why, but she seemed puzzled as she turned away without saying a word and walked out the door. White Jesus! White angels! Black man! African-centered bookstore! These images have been used as psychological weapons against Africans for some time, and as you can see, they are still being used. At the risk of sounding like an angry black man, I will state unequivocally that white Jesus and his white angels are no longer welcome in any area of my life. I know the importance of images and the impact they have on the psyche. It would be easier to sell me a lollipop for $100 than to give me a calendar with an image of a supreme being that does not look like me.

Helping Yourself

> I had to make my own living and my own opportunity . . . . Don't sit down and wait for the opportunities to come; you have to get up and make them.
>
> —Madame C. J. Walker

Madame C. J. Walker was a self-made entrepreneur who created a successful business for herself and was responsible for employing thousands of black women in the early 1900s. Her Pan-African spirit enabled her to financially support the efforts of the NAACP, the colored YMCA, the elderly, the black writers and artists, etc. Brothers and sisters, let's study the example of Madame C. J. Walker who took an idea, cultivated it, and harvested the fruits then fed her family and her community. Perhaps it is time for each of us to conduct an opportunity audit to determine what steps we are taking to create for ourselves, our family, our community, and our humanity.

A Change of Focus Is Needed

> The spirit of an ancestor has the capacity to see not only into the invisible spirit world, but also into this world, and it serves as our eyes on both sides.
>
> —Sobonfu Somé

Entertainment and entertainers dominate the spotlight in this time. In fact, we have television programs, radio programs, and magazines dedicated solely to this subject. As a society, we have become overly focused on the lives of celebrities and how they are living, making it extremely difficult to focus on anything of substance instead of the superficial. Within the African (black) community, our children are even more caught up trying to learn every made-up detail about their favorite singer, dancer, rapper, or actor/actress of the hour. There is no time to develop their creative and critical thinking skills through reading extensively, sharing of thoughts and ideas, and cultivating awareness to be able to recognize facts from fiction. It is amazing how, as a people, we have allowed the media to determine what is important to us. We do not think enough! We do not question enough! We have forgotten that we are each a mere branch of the tree. Parents and other caregivers, it is important to teach our children about their beginnings. Should your child know more about some entertainer than they know about their mother, father, grandmother, grandfather, great-grandmother, great-grandfather . . . their ancestors? Now I know many will laugh, thinking, "I cannot even tell my child about his father, how am I going to tell him about people I don't know?" The answer is simple. Africa is the cradle of civilization, it is the home of our ancestors. We have been taught many lies about Africa—forget the lies, take the time, and seek truth. For those of us who still believe in thinking, we acknowledge that many have died for us, many have lived for us—some of their names we do not know, some of their names we know, and all of them are roots to the tree of which we are a branch.

True Dedication to the Rebirth of African Civilization

> Freedom is self-affirmation, the liberty to grow and fully realize one's potential in the development of his personality, unhampered by any external authority. By its very nature, therefore, freedom involves voluntary self-commitment to some ideal, purpose and action.
>
> —As Taken from
> *The Rebirth of African*
> *Civilization* by
> Chancellor Williams

Almost as if motivated by the ancestral spirit, men such as Chancellor Williams began the process of rewriting African truths to facilitate a greater understanding of the complexities involved in African history and its ultimate destruction. Chancellor Williams dedicated sixteen years of work and research to what would eventually become the classic book, *The Destruction of Black Civilization: Great Issues of a Race from 4500 B.C. to 2000 A.D.* He did not have the resources for a well-organized research team that would include highly trained experts in archaeology, history, anthropology, medicine, linguistics, tropical agriculture, political science, etc. But he did have the assistance of over 128 Africans who understood the importance of the fieldwork that was being done to African people as a whole. This brother recognized the need for pioneering initiatives focusing on African history totally independent of Caucasians, which meant all those years of tedious, laborious, and time-consuming research also needed to be independently financed. *The Destruction of Black Civilization* gives an uncompromising view of African history from the African perspective. Chancellor outlines and explains what happened, how it happened, and provides a blueprint for what we can do as a people. This work will definitely offend those who, for various reasons, do not want to acknowledge truth; however, for those who recognize that we must all deal with some harsh truths about ourselves yesterday and today, it is a treasury that needs to be passed down from generation to generation. African people, we must create the right situation and remain in the center as much as possible, not expecting change to be brought about by any external person or situation. Let us prepare.

Honoring the Legacy of Marcus Garvey

> There is no height to which we cannot climb by using the active intelligence of our own minds. The mind creates, and as much as we desire in Nature we can have through the creation of our own minds. Self-determination is a state of mind, it is this vision that must be passed on to our youth if they are to survive the next millennium.
>
> —Marcus Garvey

On August 17, the birthday of Marcus Garvey, let us not forget to take a moment to honor his legacy, remembering his dedication to the resurrection of African people. For those of you who are proud owners of the Red, Black, and Green (Black Liberation flag or Pan-African flag), remember to display this symbol of unification and love among African people with great joy, knowing the day will come when our memories will return. For my brothers and sisters who are unaware of Marcus Garvey and the gift that he was to African people, take five minutes to read a book, search the Internet, listen to one of his speeches, or attend an event celebrating Marcus Garvey. It is never too late to learn something new and empowering.

Building Your Library One Book at a Time:
Featuring Kwame Agyei and Akua Nson Akoto

When I first arrived in Canada, most Europeans assumed that I was either African or Jamaican. Very few of the people I encountered had ever heard of Nevis. In school, I had studied the history of other islands and Jamaica—being one of the bigger ones whose historical facts I was more familiar with. I have tried to recall any studies about Africa or an existing perception in my early years without any success. It is difficult to pinpoint exactly when the negative images of savages, starving children, wild animals, and slaves started making home in my psyche. In the early '90s, on one of my return trips to Nevis, I came across the concept Sankofa that was being used as a slogan for Culturama, Nevis's carnival. Shortly after I discovered the movie *Sankofa*, I gained an understanding for this concept, and it became firmly embedded in my life. Our journey from the motherland is a very complex issue, and although Africa is in us all, our return will take a great deal of commitment and dedication to fully recover our memories. One of the books that I have thoroughly enjoyed is *The Sankofa Movement: ReAfrikanization and the Reality of War* by Kwame Agyei and Akua Nson Akoto. This book gives a comprehensive analysis of Sankofa and provides extensive terminology, definitions, concepts, and guidelines that will enhance your understanding of the movement. Now let's give Agyei and Akoto our indulgence for a moment as they explain the Sankofa movement:

> The essence of this Sankofa Movement is reAfrikanization. It is a process of return, rediscovery and recovery, rehabilitation and revitalization, spiritual and physical immersion, rebirth and recreation. The question that we often ask ourselves is the question framed in part by Fanon; that is, whether there is anything to be recovered. Has the experience of centuries of colonialism, enslavement and menticide, in addition to several millennia of self-imposed, and Asiatic/European disruption/ destruction left anything of substance, or anything beyond the "dregs of culture"? [Fanon, 1963] The fragments of tradition, and the limited or dysfunctional institutions that are still sustained in the countryside in Afrika or that are moribund in tourist sustained museums offer only fleeting clues as to those vital elements of traditional culture. The state constitutional provisions that sustain the institutions of the traditional governance in Ghana seem to rob it of its historic dynamism. The colonial inheritance of Western parliamentary state structure leeches the

traditional formation of its vitality; that is, the deep and millennia old allegiance of the people. In the Diaspora, we have even fewer fragments. Much of that which has survived has been consigned to irrelevance or sustained as exotic spectacles. Miseducation, neglect, ignorance, racism, political antipathy and the insidious and nefarious incursions of European researchers threaten to reduce the traditionalists of Surinam to tourist attractions, and the Maroons and Quilombo of Jamaica and Bahia respectively to meaningless side-shows.

In addressing this issue of cultural disintegration, it is important to recall a concept that is central to traditional Afrikan cosmology. That everything and every occurrence has a spiritual antecedent. Though a thing may be made inaccessible to material reality through some form of physical termination, it continues to exist. So it is, that though the observable features of traditional culture appears to be dismembered and beyond recovery or recognition, it can in fact be recovered.

Spirituality

Sunsum
  Symbol of spirituality, spiritual purity, and the cleanliness of the soul.

The Innermaster

> If there is something you know you should be doing but don't like doing it . . . do it anyway!
>
> —Nathan Scott

You are to be master of yourself! It is your choice to take action or not when the spirit is calling you. Most of us have probably experienced the sudden need to reach out to someone for no apparent reason, to give a helping hand, or just to do something a little different from the norm. When the Divine communicates to us through our spirit, we often allow self-imposed barriers to keep us in a place of inaction. Our greatest resource is time, and our physical journey is short, making it imperative for us to develop our ability to practice serving the innermaster. We must not give in to fear, permitting it to stop us from sharing with each other and cultivating a spirit of love.

Let Go

That was life, she said to herself. Be as cunning as a serpent and as harmless as a dove.

—Buchi Emecheta, Nigerian writer

Have you ever found yourself in a situation offering guidance and advice to someone else whose problems seem trivial or simple to solve? Being on the outside looking in, we can clearly see the solutions written right before our eyes. "You just need to focus on something positive; everything will work out just fine." When we are in the crucibles, how many of us truly have the faith and knowledge that the dark clouds will disappear and the sun will shine again? How easy is it, in that moment when we believe that things have fallen apart for us, to just let it happen and give thanks for life? We have been tricking ourselves into thinking our happiness in this existence depends upon our various addictions or attachments, making it difficult to let go of these things. Brothers and sisters, each of us is the key to our own awakening . . . The moment is yours to choose.

It's All Good

> Life kisses our faces every morning. Yet, between morning and evening,
> she laughs at our sorrows.
>
> —Khalil Gibran

We are continually encountering difficulties. We disappoint ourselves. Others disappoint us. Along the path of life, we find the self struggling to overcome hurt, anger, shame, loneliness, betrayal, resentfulness, etc. Sometimes, the things we endure are our own fault, and judgment befalls us instead of relief. Feelings of darkness, despair, and distress plague our soul as we lose sight of the Divine. Doubt arises and trust suffers. "Why," we ask, "am I in this situation?" Yet we earnestly believed that we trusted. If we truly trusted, would we question Creator as to why each of us has been blessed with our own set of unjust occurrences and unexplained lessons to deal with? Even though whatever we are experiencing may be painful, is it not true that it must be good for Creator has allowed it?

Who Can Resist Doubt and Fear?

Hearts united in pain and sorrow will not be separated by joy and happiness. Bonds that are woven in sadness are stronger than ties of joy and pleasure. Love that is washed by tears will remain eternally pure and beautiful.

—Khalil Gibran

All of us will encounter moments of doubts and times when we do not feel that we can cope with the situation at hand. These are the times when we fear not knowing what may be waiting around the corner and not being able to anticipate every danger. Our understanding is limited to our life lessons, creating chaos when we are suddenly faced with a new lesson that seems to have no purpose except to cause us pain and suffering. This is usually when the inner dialogue goes crazy with questions. Some will find the courage to admit their struggles and lack of understanding, seeking explanation through investigation. Others will be overcome by fear, always trying to play it safe, finding security in the temporal, and trying to avoid questioning the uncertain. I am fairly confident that doubts, fears, and unexpected crises will enter each of our lives at some point in time, giving us a choice of growth or death.

Are You Aware?

The wishes of the heart never arrive.

—Kikuyu

As we age, our understanding of what we can and cannot control should improve. Once the journey begins, there are no guarantees that it will turn out the way we've planned—the possibility of several unforeseen incidents taking place is likely. In the blink of an eye, we're faced with a major detour or, worse, a potentially devastating roadblock. These are interruptions that none of us can completely avoid. The question becomes, "How do we deal with these hurdles through our disappointment and frustration?" This is where it becomes important for us to realize that no matter what life throws at us, we must keep moving forward, understanding there is no road leading back to yesterday. Things will continue to happen to each of us; some we will label good, others bad. What is truly important is for us to remember that we cannot control the actions of others, nor can we foresee or predict what will happen and when it will happen to us; however, we can control what happens within ourselves.

Ask and It Shall Be Given

The ego opposes all appreciation, all recognition, all sane perception and knowledge. If you keep in mind what the spirit offers you, you cannot be vigilant for anything but God.

—*A Course in Miracles*

Have you ever been blessed to receive a resounding yes from Creator to your prayer or request? Imagine getting the green light from Creator instead of that "No, it's not my will" or "Wait, you still need to have faith and trust in me." Yes, yes, you are honored with a wonderful gift serving Creator's will. What a great moment, you got what you requested and even in greater abundance than you ever expected. Have you taken the time to acknowledge your blessing and to express gratitude for the opportunity presented to you? Sometimes, we get what we want; and then the ego comes knocking, suddenly inflating or diminishing our sense of value. In an instant, we become arrogant and selfish, no longer thankful for this precious gift that has been bestowed upon us. Our thoughts, words, and actions reduce the tremendous capability that resides in us. Stop! Be still! Listen! A lesson is taking place. You are not ordinary. Remember your power. Step into the divine self.

Don't Be Afraid to Start Where You Are

Every cause has its Effect; every Effect has its Cause; everything happens according to Law; Chance is a name for Law unrecognized; there are many planes of causation, but nothing escapes the Law.

—Taken *from Egyptian Proverbs* by Dr. Muata Ashby

I messed up! "My life is in shambles again. How could I allow my enemies to sabotage me like this? What am I going do?" Be honest. There is only one enemy, and it's you. Reserve a bit of quiet time, analyze yourself, listen to your internal chatter, discover your predominant thoughts, and don't be afraid to question yourself. We are constantly committing crimes against ourselves, not living up to our potential, allowing fear and anger to determine our actions, abusing our bodies physically and emotionally, and forgetting we are the embodiment of love. We are so conditioned to accept false information that even when our heart speaks the truth, our mind refuses to trust. Brothers and sisters, we are all in different places in our spiritual life, that is why we must start where we are and with what we have. Some of us will have to stop lying to ourselves, and others will have to stop feeding their minds negative thoughts. Until we truly know that when we look into a mirror that the image we see looking back at us is Creator, we all still have work to do.

From Darkness Came Light

Possessions vanish, and opinions change,
And passions hold a fluctuating seat:
But, by the storms of circumstances unshaken,
And subject neither to eclipse nor wane,
Duty exists.

—Taken from *Byways of*
Blessedness by James Allen

Do you ever feel like your life is lacking the necessary intensity to truly live? Do you wake up invigorated by the mere fact that your physical being has been greeted by the light of a new day filled with beauty and blessings? Truthfully, there are days when my mind is stuck in a place of weakness: I awake with my eyes and my heart close; there is no effort put forth where daily spiritual, physical, or mental exercise is concerned; and I leave the door wide open for negativity to strike at my core. Once engulfed and shackled by these negative forces, I become a prisoner of my mind, sinking deeper and deeper into the filth (abyss) created by my thoughts and actions. Then, like clockwork, anger makes its presence felt; I become angry with myself for knowing better, yet failing to do better. I find ways to punish myself for my lack of vigilance with my thoughts. In the midst of chaos, my memory returns, forcing me to struggle against death, trying my best to actively embrace life. My mind awakens me to the knowledge that life is the ultimate teacher, and my thoughts create the experiences the Divine within deems necessary for my growth. With every moment, I gain a greater understanding of life, knowing that each day greets me with light that will soon be overcome by darkness. So will be the days of my life until . . . .

The Significance of Influence

And instead of looking into the mirror each morning asking, "Mirror, mirror on the wall, am I the fairest one of all?," we should begin to ask, "Mirror, mirror on the wall, am I fooling my Black self at all?"

—Dr. Frances Cress Welsing

Everyone influences someone! Let me say it again: everyone influences someone. In any given situation, within any given group, a leader will emerge. This leader may be self-appointed, someone who strives to be distinguished as a leader, or may be someone who inherits the role due to the other personality types with in the group. Either way, someone will come to the forefront as the primary influencer. The good news is, life offers us a balance; therefore, each one of us is influencing as well as being influenced. This means that none of us is barred from being a leader or a follower. I know some of us do not wish to be labeled either as a follower or leader; however, each of us is constantly exerting influence either to bless, to uplift, to heal or to injure, to corrupt, to taint other lives. In reflecting upon my own life, I can identify different individuals who have left perceived positive and negative impressions upon my life for eternity. I am also aware of some of those lives that I have done the same to. This truth has enabled me to understand we are all equal, although some of us may shine much brighter in the spotlight.

Gratitude

The respect given to others rebounds to the giver; to deny the sacred in the Other is to deny it in oneself.

—Dr. Raymond Johnson

Why is it so difficult? What keeps us from moving beyond the uncaring "How are you doing?" and stopping to really communicate with each other like brothers and sisters? Are we just too busy to embrace each other with a genuine smile and a willingness to give all the blessings we would desire for ourselves to another? I know we live in a society that promotes individual needs, and the first question we usually pose to ourselves is, what is in it for me? Most of us have been trained to focus on the receiving aspect of life, not realizing that we get what we give. It is a reciprocal relationship. For example, I was recently invited to a friend's home for meditation and breakfast to follow. I accepted the invitation and was blessed with a beautiful start to my day. I spent the morning in a room with brothers and sisters who were laughing, sharing, being harmonious, and blessing each other with an infectious beauty that reflected their spirits. Everyone that was present received several gifts that day from Creator, including the primary source of giving the host. The first being the invitation; and all the others, including the meal, came in the form of blessings from love. Today, I give thanks to the universe for providing me with this blessing in the perfect way at the perfect time.

Unveiling the Mask

> I do not possess the truth any more than you do. Truth is what unites us in suffering and in joy. It is born of our union, in the pain and pleasure engendered there. Not you or me, but you and me. It is our common product and is a constant marvel. Its name? Wisdom.
>
> —Irénée Guilane Dioh

Is it me or my representative? If I conclude that it is the image, the concoction of the person I believe myself to be and who I would prefer others to see, then "who am I?" Each of us is simultaneously involved in several relationships at once. There are those who we have intimate attachments to, such as parents, spouses, siblings, children, partners, and close friends. Others we call community members, coworkers, and those considered strangers. Each of these relationships represents a possible source of love and support when life's problem is getting the better of us. Yet it is preferable for us to project the facade of control and strength in the presence of our loved ones, censoring our true emotions. We hide from what we wish to be, refusing to allow what we want to feel, to show, or to do what we want to do. We fear the repercussions of acknowledging our truth and the changes that will result. So then I must ask, are we genuinely ready to speak or hear truth, relinquishing all images?

Building Your Library One Book at a Time:
Featuring Dr. Wade Nobles

Dr. Wade Nobles is the executive director of the Institute for the Advanced Study of Black Family Life and Culture Inc. and one of my influences. I came across this brother once I started seeking out Pan-African psychologists and their books. I was extremely pleased to discover Dr. Nobles's groundbreaking works on African psychology connecting ancient African ideology and culture to African psychology. I have read and strongly recommend *African Psychology: Towards Its Reclamation, Reascension and Revitalization* and *Seeking the Sakhu*. Let us join Dr. Nobles on a brief journey looking at our ancestors' concept of death:

In many African tribes, a person was not considered a full human being until he had gone through the whole rhythmic process of physical birth, naming ceremony, puberty, initiation rites (sometimes in the form of ceremonial rebirth), and finally, marriage and procreation. Then, and only then, was one finally "born"—a complete person. Similarly, death initiated the systematic rhythmic process through which the person gradually was removed from the Sasa (for Africans, is the period of personal recollections of events and phenomena) to the Zamani period (Past). Hence, death and immortality have especial significance in West African traditions. After physical death, as long as a person was remembered and recognized (by name) by relatives and friends who knew him (i.e., remembered his personality, character, and words and incidents of his life), he would continue to exist in the Sasa period. When, however, the last person who knew him also died, then the former passed out of the horizon of the Sasa period and, in effect, became completely dead. He no longer had any claims to family ties. He entered into the Zamani period; that is, he became a member in the company of spirits.

The departed person who was remembered (recognized) by name was what Brother Mbiti calls the living-dead. He was considered to be in a state of personal immortality. The Mende believed that a person survives after death and that his surviving personality goes to the land of the dead. Those in personal immortality were treated symbolically like the living. The cycle of an individual ancestor, the Mende believed, lasted as long as the dead person was remembered in prayers and sacrifices. Hence, they were respected, given food and drink in the form of libations, and listened to and obeyed.

Being remembered (recognized) and respected while in personal immortality was important for the traditional African, a fact which helps one to understand the religious significance and importance of marriage and procreation in West African societies. Procreation was the surest way to insure that one would not be cut off from personal immortality. In a kind of multiplicative fashion, polygamy reinforced one's insurance.

Inevitably, as stated earlier, there was a point when there were no longer any descendants alive who could recognize and give respect to the (living-dead) person. At that point, the process of dying was completed. However, he did not vanish out of existence. He then entered into the state of collective immortality. Now in the company of the spirits, he had at last entered the Zamani period. From this point on, the departed became nameless spirits who had no personal communication or ties with human families.

In terms of the ontology, entrance into the company of the spirits is man's final destiny. Paradoxically, death lies "in front" of the individual; it is a "future" event of sorts. But, when one dies, one enters the state of personal immortality and gradually "goes back" into the Zamani period. It should be emphasized that the African ontology was endless; such a view of man's destiny should not be construed to mean the end. Nothing ever ends.

I Manifest

Gye Nyame
  "Except God."
  Symbol of the omnipotence, omnipresence, and immortality of God.
  "Except God, I fear none."

Dreams

> I have discovered in life that there are ways of getting almost anywhere you want to go, if you really want to go.
>
> —Langston Hughes

After four years of Shakespeare, Joseph Heller, Arthur Miller, Harper Lee, and numerous other European writers, discovering Langston Hughes in my final year of high school was like being reborn. The journey began . . . I read every book I could find by Langston Hughes . . . discovered James Baldwin, Maya Angelou, Walter Mosley, Frederick Douglass, Sojourner Truth, etc . . . stopped ordering black books from Coles/Smith's Bookstore once I discovered Third World bookstore . . . earned my university degree . . . walked away from a job I didn't like to follow my dreams: Knowledge Bookstore. This week, brothers and sisters, let's ask, do I really want to . . . ?

Attitude

> If there's a book you really want to read but it hasn't been written yet, then you must write it.
>
> —Toni Morrison

There comes a time in everyone's life when they must realize that they are capable of creating the life they wish for themselves. We must stop waiting for someone else to create for us! It is not a lack of knowledge that prevents us from achieving, it is our attitude—a reflection of how we decide to face our insecurities. Today, I have added another goal to my five-year plan. I am aware of the skills I must develop and the steps I will need to take. I have cleared my biggest obstacle: MYSELF. My brothers and sisters, I am in agreement with Toni Morrison, stop complaining, write the book.

Possibilities

> Impossibilities are merely things of which we have not learned, or which we do not wish to happen.
>
> —Charles W. Chesnutt

There are people who make things happen. These people discover fruits in places you thought were barren. They find potential where none existed. They create opportunities where others failed. They take something mediocre and make it extraordinary. They do not complain about the harsh lessons that come with living. They always find a way to make impossibilities opportunities. These are the people we admire. Brothers and sisters, impossibilities are merely self-imposed limitations that we have the power to shatter with our thoughts and actions.

Plan for It Today, Achieve It Tomorrow

My philosophy is that not only are you responsible for your life, but doing the best at this moment puts you in the best place for the next moment.

—Oprah Winfrey

Preparation! Preparation! Preparation! Many of us wait for life to happen. We are reactive instead of being proactive. The good news is today is a new day and you are being presented with yet another opportunity to take responsibility for yourself. Let's focus on today. Take a look at your daily agenda, does it reflect proper use of your time in order to meet future goals? If the answer is no, then you have a decision to make. It is time to start making better use of your time and stop complaining about not having enough of it. Today is invaluable and will ultimately determine your tomorrow. Brothers and sisters, let's all try making better decisions coupled with daily discipline to maximize our individual potential.

Compassion

Lose not Courage, Lose not Faith, Go Forward.

—Marcus Garvey

It is true that when things aren't right in our lives, mere words about hope, encouragement, and purpose are like uninvited guests. Once we're consumed by disappointment, hurt, and pain, words often become meaningless. We question everything, especially our existence. Our faith in a better day disappears, and our will to continue slowly fades. Deep within our heart, a fresh source of hope to go on is needed. This is when we must remember the master that resides in each of us. If we listen carefully, assurance will be provided that although the journey is filled with turmoil and suffering, we are on the correct path. To my brothers and sisters who are on their feet right now, let us not forget to show compassion for those who aren't.

The Search for Self

Truth is more than a mental exercise.

—Thurgood Marshall

Let us put away self-delusions. Recognize yourself for who you are, and see the path you are traveling as it is. You are the only person who knows the truth of your being. Prepare yourself with daily discipline to become in tune with your spirit. Learn to trust yourself in spite of your fears and what others believe you should or should not be doing. Know that there is no lazy way to truth; wrong decisions will be made and obstacles will continue to appear. See yourself as courageous as you follow your path to destiny, fulfilling your mission of truth. Disciples of truth, trust and know your quest is the divine will and purpose of Creator.

Things that Strangle Us

> Most people don't grow up. Most people age. They find parking spaces,
> honor their credit cards, get married, have children, and call that maturity.
> What that is, is aging.
>
> —Maya Angelou

Have you ever met anyone who seems to have lived several lifetimes, yet they
are the same age as you or younger? We live in a society with pre-established
measuring sticks to tell us whether we are ahead of the game or behind. Most of
us are dissatisfied with life: we just cannot seem to save enough money to buy
that house, finding that good man or woman just seems impossible, education is
getting more expensive. Whatever the reason, life is just passing us by. At some
point and time, we must each determine whether we plan to just hang around,
using up precious oxygen, or to step outside of society's restraints, accepting
responsibility for the way we use time in our current physical state. Brothers
and sisters, the universe is constantly offering us an opportunity to begin anew
and to grow. What will you do with your opportunity?

The Man in the Mirror

You cannot fix what you will not face.

—James Baldwin

One of the most challenging aspects of life is to avoid being the victim! We can always find someone or something to blame for our current condition in life. The problem is once blame is assigned elsewhere, we are no longer accountable for our personal growth or the lack of it. This is precisely the reason why it is important for us to recognize that we are constantly creating opposing forces for ourselves. Yes, in life, there are many reasons for us to be angry, ashamed, intolerant, and afraid; but we must try not to allow these emotions to cause us to betray ourselves and others. Brothers and sisters, let us be conscious that the mind is the reason for our current situation—whatever it is, that is the law.

Growth and Decay

> The man who views the world at 50 the same as he did at 20 has wasted 30 years of his life.
>
> —Muhammad Ali

It has been said that we are the sleeping people. We are trained to be faithful to our comfort zones. Yet within all that lives, there is an unstoppable urge to grow. Every human has experienced the desire to grow, whether it is physically, emotionally, spiritually, or intellectually. Unfortunately, we may find ourselves running from one religion to the next, experiencing one bad relationship after another, stuck at five feet and still not understanding quantum mechanics. Everyone is subjected to the universal law of growth or decay. This is unavoidable—it is a choice we make a preference for one over the other. Time never stands still, will you?

Universal Laws

> As long as you can find someone else to blame for anything you are
> doing, you cannot be held accountable or responsible for your growth
> or the lack of it.
>
> —Sun Bear

Each of us is responsible for the creation of the various situations within our life today. Every thought we think is another block in the building process. Our outward life and circumstances are a reflection of the quality and power of our inner thought life. Our thoughts direct the flow of activity in and out of our lives. Our mind will create our experiences. Our thoughts are our beauty, bliss, and blessings or our ugliness, sorrow, and pain. The choice is clearly ours to make. No external forces should be credited or blamed for our misfortune or prosperity. Understand the laws of the universe! Do not submit yourself as a slave and allow events to be your master! Give thanks to Creator for life and for the ability to reap our own harvest, eating of the sweet or bitter fruits of our garden.

Building Your Library One Book at a Time:
Featuring Maurice Bishop

In 1979, when Maurice Bishop and the People's Revolutionary Army overthrew the government of Grenada led by Eric Gairy, I was nine years old and still living in one of the neighboring islands, Nevis. I have vague memories of hearing about this coup on the radio and the excitement it brought to the island, just like any other political news in the region did back then. As a young child, the seriousness of the situation could not be comprehended however history is long-lived, and my chosen path has once again brought Maurice Bishop back to life in my readings and studies. In 1983, when Maurice Bishop was murdered just days before the United States invaded Grenada, I was in Canada, thirteen years old, sitting in front of the television, listening to the newscast about the invasion. I have since had the opportunity to study Maurice Bishop, who is now honored in the Pan-African museum at Knowledge Bookstore alongside Walter Rodney, Marcus Garvey, and Toussaint L'Overture. *Maurice Bishop Speaks* is a great collection of the speeches he gave as prime minister of Grenada from 1979 to 1983. Let's turn back the clock and revisit that historic moment in Grenada in 1979:

> Brothers and Sisters,
> This is Maurice Bishop speaking.
> At 4:15 a.m. this morning, the People's Revolutionary Army seized control of the army barracks at True Blue.
> The barracks were burned to the ground. After a half an hour struggle, the forces of Gairy's army were completely defeated, and surrendered.
> Every single soldier surrendered and not a single member of the revolutionary forces was injured.
> At the same time, the radio station was captured without a single shot being fired.
> Shortly after this, several cabinet ministers were captured in their beds by units of the revolutionary army.
> A number of senior police officers, including Superintendent Adonis Francis, were also taken into protective custody.
> At this moment, several police stations have already put up the white flag of surrender.
> Revolutionary forces have been dispatched to mop up any possible sources of resistance or disloyalty to the new government.

I am now calling upon the working people, the youths, workers, farmers, fishermen, middle-class people, and women to join our armed revolutionary forces at central positions in your communities and to give them any assistance which they may call for.

Virtually all stations have surrendered. I repeat, we stress, resistance will be futile.

Don't be misled by Bogo DeSouza or Cosmos Raymond into believing that there are any prospects of saving the dictator, Gairy.

The criminal dictator, Eric Gairy, apparently sensing that the end was near, yesterday fled the country, leaving orders for all opposition forces, including especially the peoples' leaders to be massacred.

Before these orders could be followed, the Peoples' Revolutionary Army was able to seize power. The people's government will now be seeking Gairy's extradition so that he may be put on trial to face charges, including the gross charges, the serious charges, of murder, fraud and the trampling of the democratic rights of our people.

In closing, let me assure the people of Grenada that all democratic freedoms, including freedom of elections, religious and political opinion, will be fully restored to the people.

The personal safety and property of individuals will be protected. Foreign residents are quite safe and are welcome to remain in Grenada.

And we look forward to continuing friendly relations with those countries with which we now have such relations.

Let me assure all supporters of the former Gairy government that they will not be injured in any way. Their homes, their families and their jobs are completely safe, so long as they do not offer violence to our government.

However, those who resist violently will be firmly dealt with. I am calling upon all the supporters of the former government to realize that Gairy has fled the country and to cooperate fully with our new government. You will not be victimized, we assure you.

People of Grenada, this revolution is for work, for food, for decent housing and health services, and for a bright future for our children and great-grandchildren.

The benefits of the revolution will be given to everyone regardless of political opinion or which political party they support.

Let us all unite as one. All police stations are again reminded to surrender their arms to the people's revolutionary forces.

We know Gairy will try to organise international assistance, but we advise that it will be an international criminal offence to assist the dictator, Gairy.

This will amount to an intolerable interference in the internal affairs of our country and will be resisted by all patriotic Grenadians with every ounce of our strength.

I am appealing to all the people, gather at all central places all over the country, and prepare to welcome and assist the people's armed forces when they come into your area. The revolution is expected to consolidate the position of power within the next few hours.

LONG LIVE THE PEOPLE OF GRENADA!

LONG LIVE FREEDOM AND DEMOCRACY!

LET US TOGETHER BUILD A JUST GRENADA! (On Radio Free Grenada at 9:48 a.m. on March 13, 1979, Maurice Bishop gave his "A bright new dawn" speech. Taken from *Maurice Bishop Speaks: The Grenada Revolution and Its Overthrow 1979-83.*)

Culture

Dono
    "The Tension-Talking Drum."
    Symbol of appellation, praise, goodwill, and rhythm.

Creating for Ourselves

Sons and Daughters of Africa arise . . . the time has come for us to pool
our resources and make ourselves a mighty race and nation.

—Marcus Garvey

Sankofa is an ancient concept that encourages internal and external
development through rediscovery, reclamation, and rebuilding of African
history and culture. The essence of Sankofa is for us to restore that which
was lost—our African self. In 1966, Maulana Ron Karenga created a
seven-day annual cultural celebration, giving people of African descent a
unique opportunity to re-establish core elements of African value systems
and traditions. This Pan-African celebration is called Kwanzaa, meaning
"first fruits." It is a time for us to show appreciation for our cultural and
historic heritage. The Nguzo Saba, the seven core principles of Kwanzaa, are
culturally and spiritually significant in reshaping our lives in our own images.
We are a people in the process of trying to rebuild ourselves, our family, and
our community, making it necessary for us to learn to put aside our petty
differences. Brothers and sisters, Kwanzaa is not a religious holiday, it is not
about your nationality, nor is it a replacement for Christmas. It is about love,
self-reliance, moral guidance, ethical values, rescuing, reconstructing . . . If
I may ask of you to take a calendar, look at the holidays highlighted. How
many of these holidays have any cultural or historical significance to us African
people? Is it not time for us to recover our memory and leave the madness
behind? For me, it is, that is why I will be focusing on the rich meaning
and message of the Nguzo Saba in my daily life and as I prepare to celebrate
Kwanzaa. If you are so inclined, please join me as the journey begins with
the first principle, *Umoja (Unity)*.

The symbols of Kwanzaa are:

- *mazao* (mah-zah'-o), the crops;
- *mkeka* (m-kay'-kah), the mat;
- *kinara* (kee-nah'-rah), the candleholder;
- *muhindi* (moo-heen'-dee), the corn;
- *mishumaa saba* (mee-shoo-mah'-ah sah'-bah), the seven candles;
- *kikombe cha umoja* (kee-kom'-bay chah oo-mo'jah), the unity cup;
- *zawadi* (zah-wah'-dee), the gifts.

Unity

> The Jews have a code, the Mohammedans have a code, and every other
> group seemingly has a code, from which they seldom depart, so as to be
> able to achieve the greatest good, especially through united action . . . .
> We need it in our business life, in our social life, in our political life, and
> as we have always said, in every phase of our activities.
>
> —Marcus Garvey

The first principle of the Nguzo Saba, Umoja (Unity), is observed and celebrated on December 26, with the center candle, the black one, being lit. Umoja (Unity) means to strive and maintain unity in the family, community, nation, and race. Maulana Karenga, the creator of Kwanzaa, defines Umoja as the foundational principle of the seven. I am in agreement! One of the most common cries in the African (black) community is unity. The problem is it needs to stop being a complaint and to start being a practice. As with everything in life, unity begins with each of us. We must practice being the example by living in harmony with our family members, community, elders, and fellow Pan-Africans. Please, don't misunderstand me. This doesn't mean the elimination of conflicts and disagreements. However, if we can manage to view each other as human equals, practice reciprocity, and develop genuine friendships based on mutual respect, then it is possible for us to avoid negative relationships. At this point, we need to commit ourselves to removing selfish behaviors and focus on mutually beneficial investments in each other's well-being, growth, and happiness. Brothers and sisters, let the practice begin.

Self-determination

> In looking forward he (the Negro) must realize that he is his own keeper and his own advocate. If he is to get anything out of life it must be the result of what he has put into it. He must put thoughtfulness, energy, determination, ambition into the affairs of life. He must not be compromising, neither must he be silly enough to think that others will do as much for him as he will do for himself. There is a disposition for the Negro to be dependent upon professed sympathy and charity from other channels. Let me say frankly that no man gives away that which is of vital value to him.
>
> —Marcus Garvey

Let us define ourselves, name ourselves, create for ourselves, and speak for ourselves instead of being defined, named, created for, and spoken for by others. The second principle of the Nguzo Saba is Kujichagulia (Self-Determination), observed on December 27, when the candle on the left side—the red one closest to the black one in the middle of the Kinara—is lit. This principle reminds us that we are a unique people with a history like no other race. Our memories are fragmented from being traumatized for hundreds of years. It is now our duty to recover these memories and get to know ourselves. African people must commit themselves to acknowledging and celebrating their strong cultural heritage, giving our children names that reflect us, developing our own businesses, and determining our value in this society. Brothers and sisters, we must practice restoring our cultural history, providing a foundation for our children, recognizing names have meaning both culturally and historically; supporting our community businesses; and speaking boldly for ourselves . . . Can we do it?

Meaning of the candles:

- Black Candle represents black people in unity.
- Red Candle represents struggle.
- Green Candle represents a fruitful future.

Collective Work and Responsibility

> How are we to confront all the dangers that even now threaten life in
> Africa—the bush fires that engulf property, the animals that threaten the
> crops, the rains that either do not come or else come at the wrong time
> and bring famine, the endemic diseases that kill or mutilate, and all the
> rest? The strongly structured, solid group remains the individual's citadel,
> the only guarantee of his meager existence. To join together is to live.
>
> —Seydou Badian

On December 28, we celebrate Ujima (Collective Work and
Responsibility), the third principle of the Nguzo Saba, with the lighting of
the first green candle. Ujima, as defined by Maulana Karenga, is "to build
and maintain our community together and make our brother's and sister's
problems our problems and to solve them together." We live in a society
where we are desensitized to each other's challenges. Our actions are often
motivated by selfish reasoning, and we frequently fail to realize there is nothing
that we can achieve on our own. We are a people, and each of our individual
problems will contribute further to the struggle that faces our community.
Brothers and sisters, we have a shared responsibility to restore that which was
damaged and destroyed: our history and our culture. If we are not prepared
to collectively work toward the liberation of African people everywhere, then
each of us will die with the knowledge that African children, including yours,
will suffer the consequences.

Kwanzaa symbols:

- Kinara (the candleholder) is symbolic of our roots, our parent
  people—continental Africans.
- Muhindi (the corn) symbolizes our children and, thus, our future
  which they embody.
- Mkeka (the mat) is symbolic of our tradition and history and, thus,
  the foundation on which we build.

Cooperative Economics

> Knowledge Bookstore, Total Sales, MACPRI, Sankofaincipher, T & T
> Quality Auto Services, Up From the Roots, Poetic Soul, A Different
> Booklist, Burke's Books, The Ashanti Room, Niahson Technologies,
> Sterling Dental Office, Carey & Associates, Too Nubian Entertainment,
> Benedicto, Plumbing/Management Maintenance Services, Ezekial Ekeh
> Financial Services, Strickly Roots, Zeddy's Auto Service, Main Optical . . .
> and many many more.
>
> —African Businesses

"To build and maintain our own stores, shops, and other businesses and to profit from them together." The fourth principle Ujamma (Cooperative Economics) is celebrated on December 29, with the lighting of a red candle. This principle emphasizes the importance of African (black) economic development. Simply said, we need to practice supporting each other. If we are to succeed in achieving self-reliance, it will be essential to have the support of the family, religious organizations, community organizations, and positive media outlets. As a community, one of our most important economic objectives should be to create opportunities for the youths. We need to continuously strive to build and to share, whether we are business owners, professionals, employees, or unemployed. Everyone has a role to play, especially since we are all consumers at some point and require the goods and services of others. Brothers and sisters, together we can make a difference.

Note: Zawadi (the gifts) is symbolic of the seeds sown by the children.

Guidelines for gift giving:

- Children are the main recipients of Kwanzaa gifts.
- The gifts are given on the basis of commitments made and kept.
- The gifts are not mandatory or excessive.

Purpose

> The nail supports the shoe, the shoe supports the horse, the horse supports
> the man, and man supports the world.
>
> —Malinke oral tradition

Hari gani? Nia. On December 30, Nia (Purpose) is celebrated with the lighting of the second green candle. The fifth principle, Nia, as defined by Dr. Karenga, is to make our collective vocation the building and developing of our community in order to restore our people to their traditional greatness. As heirs and custodians of a great cultural and historical legacy, it is now our responsibility to continue building, developing, and defending our community. Many of us are unaware of this great inheritance, while others are slowly discovering the true value of the legacy created by our ancestors. Brothers and sisters, our purpose is the continued cultivation of self, expanding upon our personal value, honoring Creator's intentions for us all to contribute to human existence, bringing good into the world . . . Harambee. Harambee. Harambee. Harambee. Harambee. Harambee. Harambee.

Meaning and pronunciation of Swahili words used during Kwanzaa:

- Hari gani? (hah-bah'-ree gah'-nee) : What's news? The response is the principle for the day.
- Harambee (hah-rahm'-bay): Let's all pull together.
- Kwanzaa yenu (kwahn'zah yay'-noo): Happy Kwanzaa.
- Nguzo Saba (en-goo'-zoh Sah'-bah): The seven principles.
- Kinara (kee-nah'-rah): Candleholder.

Creativity

> I pay homage to the point of the sun's rise, its zenith, and its setting! To the Spirits of Africa and the world! May our hands and our hearts come closer. So that, joined to the past, we may continue into the future.
> —Ritual prayer of West Africa

The sixth principle, celebrated on December 31 with the lighting of the third red candle, is Kuumba (Creativity). This principle reminds us to do always as much as we can, in the way that we can, in order to leave our community more beautiful and beneficial than we inherited it. Kuumba challenges each generation to build upon the works of previous generations. Each of us is born with a gift that we are responsible for discovering and using to the benefit of our community. Family, let us open our heart to serving those who come after; and remember, creativity provides us with an opportunity to grow, restore, and revitalize. Eternal life is yours . . . make an investment.

Faith

As we approach the end of one year and the birth of another, I give thanks
to Creator for all that has been provided in the form of Love, Beauty and
Blessings. I thank you for the gift of inspiration pass down by the ancestors.
I resolve to be free from the crippling effects of disappointments that lead to
darkness and to continually remember that I am not alone. I am grateful for
all the Love and support provided by family, friends, and community. Today
I recommit myself to the service of Creator, Knowledge and my people.

—Sean Liburd

The seventh principle is Imani (Faith), which encourages us to believe
with all our heart in our people, our parents, our teachers, our leaders, and
the righteousness and victory of our struggle. Imani, the final principle, is
celebrated on January 1, with the relighting of the previous six candles and
the last green candle. This day, being the first of a new year, presents us
with an opportunity to make an assessment of goals attained, goals still to
be achieved, and a chance to do a little self-reflection. On this day, the idea
is to reserve some time for meditation, remembering the ancestors, looking
deep into oneself, and recommitting to the belief in family, community,
people, and culture. Brothers and sisters, we have all tasted the bitter pill of
disappointment in ourselves, our family, and our community; however, as
unity brings us together, it is faith in our Creator, ourselves, our family, our
struggles, and our people that will sustain us coming together and seeing the
work through to the end . . . Harambe! Harambee! Harambee! Harambee!
Harambee! Harambee! Harambee!

Building Your Library One Book at a Time:
Featuring His Imperial Majesty Haile Selassie I

"Redemption Song," "Buffalo Soldier," "No Woman, No Cry," and "War" are just a few of Bob Marley's spectacular lineup of great hits. In the African tradition of storytelling, we use music as a means to address social issues, to make political statements, and to celebrate our rich heritage. Men like Bob Marley and Peter Tosh used the genre of reggae to tell the story of the Rastaman, to spread love, and to embrace Africa, the motherland. Today, I am putting "War" in the spotlight. Most of us are familiar with the lyrics of this song, but just in case, here it is:

What life has taught me
I would like to share with
Those who want to learn . . .

Until the philosophy which hold one race
Superior and another inferior
Is finally and permanently discredited and abandoned
Everywhere is war, me say war

That until there are no longer first class
And second class citizens of any nation
Until the colour of a man's skin
Is of no more significance than the colour of his eyes
Me say war

That until the basic human rights are equally
Guaranteed to all, without regard to race
Dis a war

That until that day
The dream of lasting peace, world citizenship
Rule of international morality
Will remain in but a fleeting illusion
To be pursued, but never attained
Now everywhere is war, war

And until the ignoble and unhappy regimes
that hold our brothers in Angola, in Mozambique,

South Africa sub-human bondage
Have been toppled, utterly destroyed
Well, everywhere is war, me say war

War in the east, war in the west
War up north, war down south
War, war, rumours of war

And until that day, the African continent
Will not know peace, we Africans will fight
We find it necessary and we know we shall win
As we are confident in the victory

Of good over evil, good over evil, good over evil
Good over evil, good over evil, good over evil

It should be known by most now that these lyrics were adapted from an excerpt of Ethiopian emperor, His Imperial Majesty Haile Selassie's address to the United Nations in October 1963. His Imperial Majesty Haile Selassie I was a deity for some, a great African leader for others, and an oppressor for yet another group; but like any other who has walked the earth in the physical and attained greatness, Emperor Haile Selassie I had loyal followers and political enemies. In any political system, there are those who benefit from the ruling party and those who suffer. Ethiopia plays a great role in the history of Africa and Africans. Haile Selassie's leadership and accomplishments make him a Pan-African and one of the greatest African leaders of our time. *Selected Speeches of His Imperial Majesty Haile Selassie I* is a collection of his speeches and gives a great insight into the mind of this celebrated leader. Here is the speech from one great mind that was made into a song by another great mind:

Mr. President, Distinguished Delegates:

Today, I stand before the world organization which has succeeded to the mantle discarded by its discredited predecessor. In this body is enshrined the principle of collective security which I successfully invoked at Geneva. Here, in this assembly, reposes the best—perhaps the last—hope for the peaceful survival of mankind.

The Charter of the United Nations expresses the noblest aspirations of man: abjuration of force in the settlement of disputes between states; the assurance of human rights and fundamental freedoms for all without distinction as to race, sex, language or religion; the safeguarding of international peace and security.

But these, too, as were the phrases of the Covenant, are only words; their value depends wholly on our will to observe and honor them and give them content and meaning.

The preservation of peace and the guaranteeing of man's basic freedoms and rights require courage and eternal vigilance: courage to speak and act—and if necessary, to suffer and die—for truth and justice; eternal vigilance, that the least transgression of international morality shall not go undetected and unremedied. These lessons must be learned anew by each succeeding generation, and that generation is fortunate indeed which learns from other than its own bitter experience. This Organization and each of its members bear a crushing and awesome responsibility: to absorb the wisdom of history and to apply it to the problems of the present, in order that future generations may be born, and live, and die, in peace.

Yet, this is the ultimatum presented to us: secure the conditions whereby men will entrust their security to a larger entity, or risk annihilation; persuade men that their salvation rests in the subordination of national and local interests to the interests of humanity, or endanger man's future. These are the objectives, yesterday unobtainable, today essential, which we must labor to achieve.

Until this is accomplished, mankind's future remains hazardous and permanent peace a matter for speculation. There is no single magic formula, no one simple step, no words, whether written into the Organization's Charter or into a treaty between states, which can automatically guarantee to us what we seek. Peace is a day-to-day problem, the product of a multitude of events and judgments. Peace is not an "is," it is a "becoming." We cannot escape the dreadful possibility of catastrophe by miscalculation. But we can reach the right decisions on the myriad subordinate problems which each new day poses, and we can thereby make our contribution and perhaps the most that can be reasonably expected of us in 1963 to the preservation of peace. It is here that the United Nations has served us—not perfectly, but well. And in enhancing the possibilities that the Organization may serve us better, we serve and bring closer our most cherished goals.

I would mention briefly today two particular issues which are of deep concern to all men: disarmament and the establishment of true equality among men. Disarmament has become the urgent imperative of our time. I do not say this because I equate the absence of arms to peace, or because I believe that bringing an end to the nuclear arms race automatically guarantees the peace, or because the elimination of nuclear warheads from the arsenals of the world will bring in its wake that change in attitude requisite to the peaceful settlement of disputes between nations. Disarmament is vital today, quite simply, because of the immense destructive capacity of which men dispose.

When we talk of the equality of man, we find, also, a challenge and an opportunity; a challenge to breathe new life into the ideals enshrined in the Charter, an opportunity to bring men closer to freedom and true equality and thus, closer to a love of peace.

The goal of the equality of man which we seek is the antithesis of the exploitation of one people by another with which the pages of history and in particular those written of the African and Asian continents, speak at such length. Exploitation, thus viewed, has many faces. But whatever guise it assumes, this evil is to be shunned where it does not exist and crushed where it does. It is the sacred duty of this Organization to ensure that the dream of equality is finally realized for all men to whom it is still denied, to guarantee that exploitation is not reincarnated in other forms in places whence it has already been banished.

As a free Africa has emerged during the past decade, a fresh attack has been launched against exploitation, wherever it still exists. And in that interaction so common to history, this in turn, has stimulated and encouraged the remaining dependent peoples to renewed efforts to throw off the yoke which has oppressed them and its claim as their birthright the twin ideals of liberty and equality. This very struggle is a struggle to establish peace, and until victory is assured, that brotherhood and understanding which nourish and give life to peace can be but partial and incomplete.

Last May, in Addis Ababa, I convened a meeting of Heads of African States and Governments. In three days, the thirty-two nations represented at that Conference demonstrated to the world that when the will and the determination exist, nations and peoples of diverse backgrounds can and will work together in unity, to the achievement of common goals and the assurance of that equality and brotherhood which we desire.

On the question of racial discrimination, the Addis Ababa Conference taught, to those who will learn, this further lesson: That until the philosophy which holds one race superior and another inferior is finally and permanently discredited and abandoned: That until there are no longer first-class and second-class citizens of any nation; That until the color of a man's skin is of no more significance than the color of his eyes; That until the basic human rights are equally guaranteed to all without regard to race; That until that day, the dream of lasting peace and world citizenship and the rule of international morality will remain but a fleeting illusion, to be pursued but never attained; And until the ignoble and unhappy regimes that hold our brothers in Angola, in Mozambique and in South Africa in subhuman bondage have been toppled and destroyed; Until bigotry and prejudice and malicious and inhuman self-interest have been replaced by understanding and tolerance and goodwill; Until all Africans stand and speak as free beings, equal in the eyes of all men, as they are in the eyes of Heaven; Until that day, the African continent will not know peace. We Africans will fight, if necessary, and we know that we shall win, as we are confident in the victory of good over evil.

Does this Organization today possess the authority and the will to act? And if it does not, are we prepared to clothe it with the power to create and enforce the rule of law? Or is the Charter a mere collection of words, without content and substance, because the essential spirit is lacking? The time in which to ponder these questions is all too short. The pages of history are full of instances in which the unwanted and the shunned nonetheless occurred because men waited to act until too late. We can brook no such delay.

Equality of representation must be assured in each of its organs. The possibilities which exist in the United Nations to provide the medium whereby the hungry may be fed, the naked clothed, the ignorant instructed, must be seized on and exploited for the flower of peace is not sustained by poverty and want. To achieve this requires courage and confidence. The courage, I believe, we possess. The confidence must be created, and to create confidence we must act courageously.

The great nations of the world would do well to remember that in the modern age, even their own fates are not wholly in their hands. Peace demands the united efforts of us all. Who can foresee what spark might ignite the fuse? It is not only the small and the weak who must scrupulously observe their obligations to the United Nations and to each other. Unless the smaller nations are accorded their proper voice in the settlement of the world's problems, unless the equality which Africa and Asia have struggled to attain is reflected in expanded membership in the institutions which make up the United Nations, confidence will come just that much harder. Unless the rights of the least of men are as assiduously protected as those of the greatest, the seeds of confidence will fall on barren soil.

The stake of each one of us is identical—life or death. We all wish to live. We all seek a world in which men are freed of the burdens of ignorance, poverty, hunger and disease. And we shall all be hard-pressed to escape the deadly rain of nuclear fall-out should catastrophe overtake us.

When I spoke at Geneva in 1936, there was no precedent for a head of state addressing the League of Nations. I am neither the first, nor will I be the last head of state to address the United Nations, but only I have addressed both the League and this Organization in this capacity. The problems which confront us today are, equally, unprecedented. They have no counterparts in human experience. Men search the pages of history for solutions, for precedents, but there are none. This, then, is the ultimate challenge. Where are we to look for our survival, for the answers to the questions which have never before been posed? We must look, first, to Almighty God, Who has raised man above the animals and endowed him with intelligence and reason. We must put our faith in Him, that He will not desert us or permit us to destroy humanity which He created in His image. And we must look into ourselves, into the depth of our souls. We must become something we have never been and for which our education and experience and environment have ill-prepared us. We must become bigger than we have been: more courageous, greater in spirit, larger in outlook. We must become members of a new race, overcoming petty prejudice, owing our ultimate allegiance not to nations but to our fellow men within the human community.

Emperor Haile Selassie, Bob Marley, Ethiopia, Jamaica, Rasta, locks, and reggae music are all part of our great African culture and history. The written word and the spoken word are and will forever be a part of our African traditions. We have forgotten many things, making it difficult to make connections to the root. If we would examine Africans spread across the globe, we will encounter more similarities in culture, behavior, and challenges than differences. We are one people.

Naked

Mate masie.
   "What I hear, I keep" (i.e., I understand).
   Symbol of wisdom, knowledge, and prudence.

My Prayer

Creator, hear my prayer tonight, it is coming straight from my heartbeat.
I thank you for the breath of life.
I thank you for good health.
I thank you for the blessing of love that surrounds me.

Creator, hear my prayer tonight, it is coming straight from my heartbeat.
I thank you for family, friends, and community.
I thank you for knowledge and the ability to learn.
I thank you for wealth and strength.

Creator, hear my prayer tonight, it is coming straight from my heartbeat.
I thank you for the ancestors and their example.
I thank you for awaking me from my slumber.
I thank you for the memories, lessons, and future hopes.

Creator, hear my prayer tonight, it is coming straight from my heartbeat.
I thank you for your guidance and ask that you never let me forget we are one.
I thank you for the Divine that is me.
I thank you for placing yourself in everything that surrounds me.

Creator, hear my prayer tonight, it is coming straight from my heartbeat.
Thanks and praises to the Creator and everything in nature.
Thanks and praises to the ancestors who live within me.
Thanks and praises to my divine self.

Creator, hear my prayer tonight, it is coming straight from my heartbeat.
I ask that you keep my spirit humble, that I may live my purpose in service of my people.
I ask that you continue to give me strength to overcome the negative forces of my ego.
I ask that you continue to open my memory to the meaning of love, peace, and happiness.
Creator, hear my prayer tonight, it is coming straight from my heartbeat in appreciation of all your blessings.

Oneness

> If I didn't define myself for myself, I would be crunched into other people's fantasies for me and eaten alive.
>
> —Audre Lorde

The Creator has blessed us with free will, the ability to think critically and make decisions. My evolution has been a combination of choices that has led me to destiny. I have learned to embrace the gift of choice as my greatest source of self-determination. Knowing that thoughts manifest into acts and repeated acts become habits and habits become unconscious actions, I am aware of the process of creating my character. With this knowledge and the fact that I am a changing, evolving, being, my life is guided by the proverb "Know thyself, love thyself, and serve thyself." Brothers and sisters, I encourage you to join me in striving for oneness.

Finishing

It's not over until you win.

—Les Brown

On Sunday, June 4, 2006, I joined a friend as we both participated in the annual ride for heart for the first time. As we made our way to the starting line at 6:35 a.m., we decided it might be best to do the 25 km instead of the 50 km since both of us had a late night and she was suffering the effects of a cold. We had an enthusiastic start riding on the Gardiner Expressway—what a beautiful feeling. No cars to worry about, just a whole lot of space for us bikers. The path now seemed easier than anticipated. It wasn't long before I started hearing gears shifting . . . You guessed it, the first hill. I expected a couple of hills. What I didn't expect was one hill after the other after the other. As we approached 12.5 km, the turnaround point, my friend decided she was good for the 50 km. The challenge of finishing another 37.5 km could now be seen clearly by me. I knew that I was about to break more than the usual sweat battling the hills that lay before me, and my discipline would have to be at its best to overcome my fatigue. Brothers and sisters, the thought of meeting this personal challenge and crossing the finish line made me smile as I continued my ride.

Illusions

This I know is true, truth is accepted by only a few.
—Taken from *Passages from Life*
by the Soul Adventurer

My love, I must confess I am like you. I too clothed myself in images of protection. Life has provided me with masks to match each occasion. Your ears hear words that my mind knows aren't true. My appearance conceals the hurt of my heart. Years of practice has made me skilled at avoiding full disclosure. I am safe. Yes, to be someone I am not. To avoid cultivating an atmosphere of openness that will allow me to share my innermost being, my hopes, my fears, and my goals in an unguarded manner. No! I cannot allow another's inability to accept me as I am to condemn me to wear a mask of hypocrisy. My love, I must accept me.

Confessions

> I am the eternal spirit; I am the sun that rose from primeval waters. My soul my spirit, my melanin is God. I am the Creator of the word. Evil is my abomination. I see it not. I am the Creator of the order wherein I live. I am the word which will never be annihilated and this my name of soul.
>
> —Taken from *Seeking the Sakhu* by Wade W. Nobles

The last several weeks have been some of the most challenging of my life. I have experienced a wide range of emotions: shock, elation, intense anger, serenity, disillusionment, contentment, and ecstasy. I have read more, wrote more, and taken more time for myself trying to master my thoughts, eliminating my natural human tendency to emphasize on the negative events in my life. Over the years, I have grown to realize that the only true battle is for the mind. In trying to apply the principle of controlling my thoughts, I am learning to confront myself, tenderly acknowledging my bad habits, knowing that there is also the positive qualities that combine to make me—the whole person. When something happens that I can't understand, that shakes me to the core, draining my reserve of happiness. Grief finds a home. These are the times I must dig deep, seeking faith to free myself from resentment of self-inflicted chastisement. I am continuously striving to cultivate daily rituals designed to reinforce my devotion to a higher purpose. Still, I find myself fighting back tears in the most unexpected moments as I quietly continue my journey with an awareness and understanding of the visible and invisible.

No Labels Please

African knowledge of God is expressed in proverbs, short statements, songs, prayers, names, myths, stories and religious ceremonies. All these are easy to remember and pass on to the other people, since there are no sacred writings in traditional societies. One should not, therefore, expect long dissertations about God. But God is no stranger to African peoples, and in traditional life there are no atheists. This is summarized in an Ashanti proverb that "No one shows a child the Supreme Being." That means that everybody knows of God's existence almost by instinct, and even children know him.

—Taken from *African Religions and Philosophy* by John S. Mbiti

I am the youngest of my father's nineteen children. I have over forty nephews and nieces, a few that are older than me, several that are my age group, and a whole lot that are much younger than me. I was raised in a Christian household. My mother has been a born-again Christian from my earliest memory. My father knew his Bible better than most pastors, and he attended church occasionally. I have been a regular churchgoer and an infrequent visitor. I have read through the Bible three times completely and studied various books of the Bible. I have also questioned the contents of the Bible. Most of my siblings are older now, and most of them have accepted Jesus as their lord and savior. I have not! It is my understanding that religion is an organized system of faith and worship. In each religion, there are many different sects, as a result of various differences in beliefs, organizational structure, politics, and interpretations of religious texts. I believe in a Creator of all things, I believe that Creator exists in all of creation, and I do not believe in the need to label myself as Christian, Muslim, Buddhist, Hebrew, Taoist, etc., in order for me to worship Creator. Each acknowledgement I express of thanksgiving for the breath of life is offering reverence to Creator. Every time I show love to myself, my brothers, and my sisters, I am worshipping Creator. And each time I am able to see the beauty that exists all around me, I am one with Creator. Unlike the rest of my family members, I have not labeled myself a Christian, for there is no need. I will not condemn Christianity or those who choose to practice it. I believe the church has provided African people with great hope, although I wish it was hope for this lifetime instead of the other, but it is hope nonetheless. Institutions like churches can help to empower Africans if the leaders and decision makers deem it beneficial. Creator has granted us all free choice. Please be content with your choice of religion for I am with mine, the way I live my life, revealing all.

The Beginning of a Journey

> I have learned it is necessary in life to take a moment to acknowledge
> and give thanks to those who came into my life for a reason, a season or
> a lifetime. Each of these people is partly responsible for who I am today.
> I understand that Creator makes no mistakes and give thanks today for
> blessings I failed to recognize yesterday.
>
> —Sean Liburd

I would like to say thanks to Mrs. Morton, my thirteenth-grade English teacher, who took the time to pull me aside and suggest that I consider doing my independent studies project on Langston Hughes, James Baldwin, Toni Morrison, or Alice Walker. Although I was an avid reader at that time, I was not familiar with any of these writers. I followed her suggestion and spent some time at the public library researching each of the writers. After reading a paragraph from one of his *Simple* books, Langston Hughes became a quick favorite. For the first time in my five years of high school, I was looking forward to doing an oral presentation to my classmates. My presentation consisted of a brief biography of Langston Hughes, performing two of his poetry pieces that I had committed to memory and acting out a scene from *The Best of Simple*, speaking about the conditions facing black people at that time. The week of my presentation, Mrs. Morton was out sick. Although she had the substitute teacher tape-record all the presentations, it was a bit disappointing that she was not present. I did my presentation in front of a class of over thirty European students and two African students, highlighting all the evil deeds their ancestors committed against mine. At the end, I got several questions from my white classmates, not one of them seemed offended. The two black students who had never spoken to me before actually approached me afterward and expressed their appreciation and even requested a copy of my written portion of the project. Upon her return, Mrs. Morton requested my presence after class where she took the time to congratulate me on a job well done. She also shared her experience from the civil rights days and forewarned me about the challenges that lied ahead for a young black man like myself. Reflecting back, I realize Mrs. Morton was also my English teacher in grade 11 and had also paid quite a bit of attention to all of the black male students. She had also agreed to be our track and field coach when no other teacher would enable us to have a team. This European teacher, who just happened to be married to a black judge, impacted my life in a profound way simply by pointing me in the direction of self-knowledge and self-love.

A Heartfelt Loss

> It is normal and even necessary that the arrival of a newborn bring a
> change in the relationship of the parents. As mothers we have to build
> an intimate relationship with the baby while it is still in the womb and
> continue to nourish this relationship after birth. It is the responsibility of
> the father to develop a relationship with the child also. Unless both parents
> are closely tied to the child and, along with that, keep their relationship
> between each other healthy, somebody will feel left out.
>
> —Taken from *The Spirit of*
> *Intimacy* by Sobonfu Somé

Expectation leads to disappointment. This is one of life's truths that I learned some time ago. The problem is that I have yet to learn how to live without having expectations. After finding out my wife was pregnant, I fully expected to be a father to a baby girl in a matter of months. I cautiously embraced the fact that one of the ancestors chose me to be one of her guardians to guide her in her journey back into this physical realm. My anticipation of the endless possibilities associated with this impending birth brought high expectations for my unborn child. Within a short period of time, she became Zula. There was no room for doubt. I knew my wife was carrying a female child. Being aware of the natural bonding advantage of a mother and the negative perceptions of the black man as a father, I immediately assumed my role. Daily rituals were established that involved nightly reading, prayer, conversations, and exposure to an array of music, including my developing guitar skills. In an instant, everything changed. Emergency! Hospital! Triage! Waiting! More waiting! Doctor! Relief! I silently gave thanks to Creator after hearing Zula's heartbeat and was happy to return home where my wife could rest comfortably.

Thirteen hours later, back to emergency! Trying to keep fear at bay! Crowded waiting room! Chaos! Memories of the hours spent in this same waiting room with my sick father flooded my mind. I struggled to remain present. Family arrived, we waited and waited. Time elapsed, my wife was seen. My sister told me what I already knew; Zula was no more. I took a few minutes to allow my tears free reign and to find the strength to be a source of support for my wife. The days that followed brought great emotional pain and well-meaning supporters of which some just did not understand there was no need for too many words but just a simple hug would suffice. This kind of loss is fairly common, and pain is personal; therefore, we must each deal with our emotions in our own fashion. As for me, I understand there is a time for everything, and Creator has decided Zula was not to come forth. Even with this understanding, I still experience moments of anger, periods of questioning, and constant introspection for the hope I had for this child will never materialize . . . Now, healing is a matter of time.

Building Your Library One Book at a Time:
Featuring Dr. Na'Im Akbar

As I travel through this journey called life, the importance of guarding your mind against certain kind of influences has become clearer and clearer. Growing up in this society, I never thought I would see the age of twenty. The media got into my mind at an early age, telling me that as a young black male, I was likely to die a violent death before getting out of my teens. Reflecting back, I realize that I lived a very sheltered life. I was never around violent people, violent situations, or criminal activities. The chances of me dying through violent means as a young black male were minimal. Books have been a blessing to me, and men like Dr. Na'Im Akbar have been embraced as my teacher. Brother Akbar deals with the mind and helping African people to face our circumstances by getting to know ourselves and empowering ourselves.

I have thought of myself as a man for some time now. I have always seen myself as a responsible individual with goals and a purpose. I believe that I was and am doing what I am supposed to be doing to earn the title. Dr. Akbar made me question this after reading *Visions for Black Men*. He outlines the difference between a male, a boy, and a man:

> A male, a boy, and a man are not the same thing. A male is a biological creature, a boy is a creature in transition, and a man is something that has arrived to a purpose and destiny. When men become real men and do not confuse their maleness or their boyishness with their manliness, they have come into a true rediscovery of what they are. There are problems with those who confuse their biological functions with their spiritual function as men. There are problems with "boys" who think they're men—who enjoy playing games, who enjoy riding in fast cars, who enjoy listening to loud music, who enjoy running after women, and who enjoy running real fast rather than being steady and directed as men are.

I have tried my best to identify aspects of myself that need my attention. It is difficult for me to look at myself and admit that I am covering up my truths with facades. In reading *Visions for Black Men*, I can admit that I saw some of the boyish behaviors in myself. I am not big on fast cars or cars, period. They serve a simple purpose for me: getting from point A to B. Music I enjoy. Playing my music loud while driving, for me, is not about the enjoyment, it is about blocking my thoughts and escaping from the things I need to deal with. In silence, there is no distraction. I cannot hide from the voice of Creator. I know the things that I struggle to overcome, the parts of my life that are undisciplined, and the mistakes that I make over and over again. Although I have been practicing self-improvement for quite some time before being introduced to Dr. Akbar's works, he has been instrumental in helping me to be more in-depth in my self-examination. I have also gained a better understanding of my African people and humans, helping me to refrain from being too judgmental in my assessment of others. *Visions for Black Men* highlights various behaviors that the brothers need to address and the importance of the transformation process:

> What is the process by which we are able to transcend the destructiveness of our current situation and move into the horizon where we belong and where we need to be going? This is a time when African men are more needed than they've ever been. The need for real men in this world is greater than it has ever been in our history in North America, and probably in our continuing history as a people. One of the beautiful things that we understand is that "nature," as the vehicle for the Creator, has the ability to bring into being whatever is needed, when it is needed. Even though we are suffering now from this deficit of men with the qualities that we're going to describe, we understand that we have faith in the process that is operative, in a process that is real, in a process that is genuine, in a process that is inescapable—by which that which is needed is brought into being. You will have faith in the process once you understand the process by which all vacuums in nature are filled. Once the vacuum of manly leadership coming from the origin of human leadership has been restored, then the solutions have arrived.

The African community has always faced challenges, African men have always faced challenges, and Creator has always provided hope for a better tomorrow. Our history is filled with men sent forth for the purpose of uplifting humanity. I respect the example of Marcus Garvey, Stephen Bantu Biko, Langston Hughes, Dr. John Henrik Clarke, and Martin Luther King Jr. These men dedicated their lives to a purpose and, in some cases, died for that purpose. All of these men faced personal challenges in their lives whether it was drinking, womanizing, arrogance, depression, etc. Did their personal demons take away from the contribution they made to the African community? Absolutely not! If we were to take the time and strip away our layers, allowing ourselves to be naked for just a moment, we would discover that we tend to hold others to a standard that we ourselves cannot meet. Dr. Akbar has provided me with some additional standards to strive for; and I am going to try, knowing that it will take time and commitment, especially when I find myself holding on to old habits.

Community: Redefined

Fi-Hankare.
"An enclosed or secured compound house."
Symbol of brotherhood, safety, security, completeness, and solidarity.

Branches of the Same Tree

Once you put all the purely African people or people of African descent together . . . you've got a formidable force in the world. And what keeps them from greatness is their inability to unify their culture and make a connection to Africa.

—Taken from *Africans at the Crossroad: Notes for an African World Revolution* by John Henrik Clarke

The one fact that we are certain about in life is that we will all die physically. Yet when death comes calling, we still ask, "Why me? Why is this happening to me?" I recently read somewhere that Les Brown asks, "Why not you? Would you prefer for it to happen to someone else?" Honestly speaking, I do believe we would. More often than not, we are desensitized to other people's problems and hurts. Life is okay as long as Creator opens that door of pain for someone else outside of our circle of love. We are no longer a village, a tribe, or even a community that acknowledges that we are branches of the same tree; and when something bad happens to one branch, the whole tree could potentially be at risk. If African people could truly understand the importance of building foundations, recognizing and repairing cracks in those foundations together, it would drastically improve our spiritual powers. Growing up in the Caribbean, I can remember numerous examples of people working together, giving each other a helping hand. On my visits back to Nevis, I was always encouraged, within the first twenty-four hours on the island, to visit each of the elders and our neighbors to pay my respects. If those of us from the Caribbean would take a minute, we would realize that we were able to retain some of our African traditions. Unfortunately, we are still losing our memories and will continue to unless steps are taken to reunite our spirits.

It's Up to Me to Do It and Live It

The mere breaking of the chains of bondage only free an individual or a people mentally and physically. What is done from that point on determines whether they are actually free.

—Taken from *The Rebirth of African Civilization* by Chancellor Williams

Have you ever wondered if it is too late for African people to regroup, refocus, and rebuild our nation economically, spiritually, politically, and even militarily? It seems unreal at times when I sit and ponder ancient African civilizations and their accomplishments. Imagine mining your own natural resources alongside your fellow community members, bartering and supporting each other in a place where no one owns the land. Relax, open your mind to the possibility of what it was like to practice indigenous African religions through rituals, ceremonies, festivals, oral traditions, or just simply in your heart and mind. Are you still with me? Let's forget about going to the polls, no need for any political parties. We have elders, those who possess life's knowledge, coming together as a council that is available to the community 24/7 for guidance, instructions, and solutions. I'm about to keep it real. This scenario is definitely going to include some form of protection for the community—whether it is trained warriors, combat ready no matter what form the enemy takes, or physical protection that ensures a level of safety for the people. Stay with me just a little longer. The above scenario is by no means the only one. Africa was and is a very diverse place. Another scenario may include prayers, invocations, blessings, salutations, sacrifices, offerings, spirits, tribes, kings, queens, initiations, rites of passage, gold, oil, coffee, pyramids, guards, armies, hunting parties, etc. I could go on and on presenting our rich heritage. Okay, back to the present. African people are scattered all over the world, serving everyone else's purpose other than our own. Some of you probably answered no to the question originally posed, others are probably indifferent and don't care either way, and some of us still have enough hope to say, "Yes, it can be done." History is constantly unfolding and teaching us valuable lessons. I have learned that African people moved away from their traditions, culture, beliefs, or simply themselves. The truth is all we need to recapture ourselves is one person to know it is possible. There is no need to worry about the majority for they will always follow. All it takes is the power of one . . . will it be you?

The Foundation: Family

How can we move towards a more sane family structure or relationship structure? The main thing I see at this point is community—building communities where you can trust one another, where you can help a mother who is crying because she has a child who is crying and she doesn't know what to give her.

—Taken from *The Spirit of
Intimacy* by Sobonfu Somé

We are emotional beings! At some point in time, we have all experienced feelings of love, happiness, anger, sadness, and fear. These are the major categories of emotions that drive us to seek or avoid relationships. All of us have had a desire for some form of intimacy. Within the human spirit is a natural instinct for casual interaction, companionship, friendship, and spiritual or sexual union. We often attempt to fulfill our urges without taking the time to understand what we are truly searching for. We confuse love, sex, romance, and friendship. We learn about relationships from our immediate environment: caregivers, television, books, or just the society we live in. Our concept about and how we perceive love and relationships are all derived from environmental factors. Religion and culture are also guiding forces in how we approach and develop relationships. Traditions of old are no longer valued. Family once played a pivotal role in African social order. It was the primary source of education, economics, and politics. Families were the foundation of communities. Men and women coming together in marriage were never solely about individual needs alone, it also incorporated the needs of the community. Couples having children were also about community building. In today's society, we are faced with many distractions and weapons of mass programming, making it extremely challenging to view relationships as an opportunity for everyone involved, including our community, to grow.

Fathers Are Always Needed

We must begin at the cradle and teach our babies that they must do something for self. They must not be like we, their fathers, who look to the slave-makers' and slave-master's children for all. We must teach our children now with an enthusiasm exceeding that which our slave-masters used in having our forefathers imbed the seed of dependency within us. We must stop the process of giving our brain power, labor and wealth to our slave-masters' children. We must eliminate the master-slave relationship.

—Taken from *Message to the Blackman in America* by Elijah Muhammad

I grew up in a two-parent household, with a full-time mother and a working father. I saw my father put forth a great effort in being available for all of his children in the best way he knew how to. I have watched my older brothers becoming a part of their children's lives whether or not they were married to the mothers, and I have eight brothers. Being a witness not only to the men in my family but also to most men that I am closely associated to stepping up and being a father to their children, I am sometimes puzzled when I hear others complaining about black men not taking care of their children. I realize these issues are usually more complex than most are willing to say, and like the man said, there are three sides to every story. Statistics tells us that children raised without fathers are "more likely to drop out of school, to get pregnant as teenagers, to abuse drugs, and to be in trouble with the law." I could continue quoting more negative statistics of not having active fathers, but I am hoping you got the point. My brother's children are a huge part of our legacy. We need to make sure our children know from before birth their value to us, which means a serious commitment to being a part of their lives no matter what. For those brothers without children, don't be afraid of being a father to a child without one—someone has to. It would be great if all of our children could have fathers that are willing to create special time for them. However, if this ideal is too great, then hopefully a majority of fathers will. Many of us don't have a clue of how to be a good father. This we need to forget and focus on what type of father we would like to be. As always, be prepared to make mistakes. For my sisters, please allow my brothers to be fathers, don't punish your children for your choices.

You Can't Blame the Youth

> You teacher used teach about Pirate Hawkins
> you teacher used teach about Pirate Morgan
> And you said he was a very great man
> you teacher used teach about Christopher Columbus
> And you said he was a very great man
> you teacher used teach about Marco Polo, so
> You can't blame the youth
> You can't fool the youth
> You can't blame the youth of today.

> —Lyrics from "You Can't
> Blame the Youth"
> by Peter Tosh

Every February for the last ten years, I have had the privilege of going into schools for Black History Month celebrations. Each year, without fail, there is a couple of cultural shows with the highlight being some form of hip-hop dancing and a fashion show. I will be the first to admit I love music. I indulge in reggae, calypso, jazz, blues, soul, African drumming, and plenty of other genres. In my senior years of high school, I did some modeling outside of school. I have also done my share of dancing and still do as a form of celebrating. I share this with you to keep things real when I say our children need to become more creative in these presentations. Yes, dancing is a part of our culture, and it's fun and so is a fashion show; but how about mixing things up a bit? Why not a skit or a play about some of the ancestors, keeping their memory alive? What is Black History Month really about? Okay, here come the stones, why can't the black teachers work with these students to create an evening more representative of our great African history? Well, I got some bad news, the black teachers are usually as ignorant as the students about their history. No, no, no, don't you go jumping on the bandwagon with me 'cause, parents, I'm getting to you. Where is the parent that is supposed to be at these shows, supporting their children's effort? Usually, nowhere to be found! Well, if you are not at the shows, what do you expect from these children? How are you going to give feedback? I hear a lot of complaints about the youths and what they are doing, as well as what they are not doing. I see parents bring their children into the bookstore and try to force them to get a book to read then stand at the counter telling me they have not read a book in many years. I usually just smile and patiently wait for my opening before asking one simple question, "Why do you expect your child to read when you are not providing the example they need?" We see the issues: youth violence, teenage pregnancies, high dropout rates, and the list goes on. Yes, these are problems we must confront as a community along with our children's ignorance about themselves. In the final analysis, I will have to agree with Peter Tosh's "You Can't Blame the Youth." If you think the youths of today is a problem, then know that you are a problem.

Building Your Library One Book at a Time: Featuring Ishakamusa Barashango

In 1998, I picked up the phone and dialed Barashango's number. Within minutes, he answered, and we quickly got lost in conversation. I listened and he spoke. After hanging up the phone, it occurred to me that I had just received a lesson from a pillar of the community. Over the next six years, I got more familiar with Rev. Barashango's work by collecting and listening to his lecture series on audio, watching his videotape presentations and reading his books. After recognizing the importance of what Barashango had to offer, I started working on bringing him to Toronto for a lecture in late 2003. Unfortunately for us all, Barashango transitioned on January 14, 2004—ironically, a mere ten days after Dr. Jacob Carruthers had departed this physical realm. Dr. Barashango dedicated his life to the spiritual, mental, and physical liberation of African people. He gave us two volumes, exposing the truth behind European holidays, entitled *Afrikan People and European Holidays : A Mental Genocide, Book One and Two*. He also left us *Afrikan Genesis: Amazing Stories of Man's Beginnings*, explaining various creation myths and their purpose. For those who appreciate truth, these books are rare treasures. Dr. Barashango explains the reasons for his work:

> Our daily prayer is that more and more Afrikan people from every walk of life, wherever we are in the world today will continue to organize and institute study groups and from these satellite bases establish research centers, community libraries, museums and even Afrikan-centered institutions of higher learning. Fortunately, you do not have to start out big to do this. All that is needed is a few sincere committed Brothers and Sisters who will lovingly join forces on a consistent basis, pool their resources, obtain a space, even if it is no more than a store front and build from there. You may be amazed at how far you can go with this once you set your mind to it. In fact there are already many such efforts in progress in many Afrikan communities. Most of them would be more than happy to network with you. Lord knows we certainly have an enlightened army of scholars and brain trusts to provide information and guidance for these endeavors.
>
> Again I would remind you that Black people from all walks of life can participate in this process. What a glorious undertaking. What a marvelous vitality and positive stimulus this would/will bring to our

community. For once the Black Race begins to obtain a sufficient and proficient "knowledge of self," it will be just a matter of time before many of us will be about the business of collectively transforming our communities and moving our race further along the high road of our rightful place in the sun. Helping to keep this idea alive and encouraging its fruition is the sacred goal and mission of Fourth Dynasty Publishing Company, as we strive to "attain victory in concert with other Afrikans of like mind and spirit."

Asante, brothers and sisters, it has been a pleasure traveling the road of life with you. It is my heart's wish that we may continue the journey together; however, if it is not to be, let us part with the knowledge that this is not an end, but merely a beginning of the next chapter in the book of life.

The journey continues . . .

Building Your Library One Book at a Time

Featuring 100 Great Nonfiction Books Read and Recommended by Sean Liburd

1. *When We Ruled* by Robin Walker
2. *The Destruction of Black Civilization* by Chancellor Williams
3. *The African Origins of Civilization: Myth or Reality* by Cheikh Anta Diop
4. *Africa: Mother of Western Civilization* by Dr. Yosef A. A. ben-Jochannan
5. *Blackman of the Nile and His Family* by Dr. Yosef A. A. ben-Jochannan
6. *A Chronology of the Bible* by Dr. Yosef A. A. ben-Jochannan
7. *African Glory: The Story of Vanished Negro Civilization* by J. C. DeGraft-Johnson
8. *Stolen Legacy* by G. M. James
9. *Nile Valley Contribution to Civilization* by Anthony T. Browder
10. *They Came Before Columbus* by Ivan Van Sertima
11. *Introduction to African Civilizations* by John G. Jackson
12. *Blacks in Antiquity* by Frank M. Snowden Jr.
13. *What They Never Told You in History Class* by Indus Khamit-Kush
14. *World's Great Men of Color, Volume 1 and 2* by J. A. Rogers
15. *100 Amazing Facts about the Negro with Complete Proof* by J. A. Rogers
16. *African Presence in Early Asia* by Runoko Rashidi
17. *The African Origins of Civilization, Religion, Yoga Mystical Spirituality and Ethics Philosophy* by Dr. Muata Abhaya Ashby
18. *Wonderful Ethiopians of the Ancient Cushite Empire* by Drusilla Dunjee Houston
19. *Yurugu: An African-centered Critique of European Cultural Thought and Behavior* by Marimba Ani
20. *Afrocentric Idea* by Molefi Asante
21. *How Europe Underdeveloped Africa* by Walter Rodney
22. *Afrikan Genesis : Amazing Stories of Man's Beginnings* by Ishakamusa Barashango

23. *Afrikan People and European Holidays : A Mental Genocide Book One and Two* by Ishakamusa Barashango
24. *African Intellectual Heritage: A Book of Sources* by Molefi Kete Asante and Abu S. Abarry
25. *Maurice Bishop Speaks: The Grenada Revolution and its Overthrow 1979-83* by Maurice Bishop
26. *Thomas Sankara Speaks: The Burkina Faso Revolution 1983-87* by Thomas Sankara
27. Selected Speeches of His Imperial Majesty Haile Selassie I
28. *Capitalism and Slavery* by Eric Williams
29. *Breaking the Chains of Psychological Slavery* by Na'im Akbar
30. *Vision for Black Men* by Na' im Akbar
31. *The Isis Papers* by Dr. Frances Cress Welsing
32. *Post Traumatic Slave Syndrome* by Joy DeGruy-Leary
33. *Intellectual Warfare* by Jacob H. Carruthers
34. *SBA: The Reawakening of the African Mind* by Asa G. Hilliard III
35. *Seeking the Sakhu: Foundational Writings for an African Psychology* by Wade W. Nobles
36. *African Psychology: Towards its Reclamation, Reascension and Reevitalization* by Wade W. Nobles
37. *Blueprint for Black Power* by Amos Wilson
38. *A Black Parent's Handbook to Educating Your Children* by Baruti K. Kafele
39. *Awakening the Natural Genius of Black Children* by Amos N. Wilson
40. *Kill Them Before They Grow: The Misdiagnosis of African American Boys in America's Classrooms* by Michael Porter
41. *Bringing the Black Boy to Manhood: The Hare Plan* by Nathan and Julia Hare
42. *To Be Popular or Smart : The Black Peer Group* by Jawanza Kunjufu
43. *Motivating and Preparing Black Youth for Success* by Jawanza Kunjufu
44. *Developing Positive Self-Images and Discipline in Black Children* by Jawanza Kunjufu
45. *The Warrior Method: A Parents' Guide to Rearing Healthy Black Boys* by Raymond Winbush
46. *Message to the People* by Tony Martin
47. *The Philosophy and Opinions of Marcus Garvey* by Amy Jacques Garvey

48. *Autobiography of Malcolm X* by Alex Haley
49. *Roots* by Alex Haley
50. *The Souls of Black Folks* by W. E. B. DuBois
51. *Up from Slavery* by Booker T. Washington
52. *The Hanging of Angélique : The Untold Story of Canadian Slavery and the Burning of Old Montréal* by Afua Cooper
53. *Narrative of the Life of Frederick Douglass : An American Slave* by Frederick Douglass
54. *The Mother of Us All: A History of Queen Nanny, Leader of the Winward Jamaican Maroons* by Karla Gottlieb
55. *The Black Jacobins : Toussaint L'Ouverture and the San Domingo Revolution* by C. L. R. James
56. *The Mis-Education of the Negro* by Carter G. Woodson
57. *The Spirit of Intimacy: Ancient African Teachings in the Ways of Relationships* by Sobonfu Somé
58. *Ritual: Power, Healing, and Community* by Malidoma Patrice Somé
59. *African Religions and Philosophy* by John S Mbiti
60. *Choosing Life: Guidelines to Avoiding Extinction* by Michael C. Frost
61. *The Sankofa Movement* by Kwame Agyei and Akua Nson Akoto
62. *The Spirit of a Man: A Vision of Transformation for Black Men and the Women Who Love Them* by Iyanla Vanzant
63. *Acts of Faith: Daily Meditations for People of Color* by Iyanla Vanzant
64. *Kwanzaa: A Celebration of Family, Community and Culture* by Maulana Karenga
65. *The Meaning of Blackness* by Im Nur
66. *African Origin of Biological Psychiatry* by Richard King
67. *Melanin* by Richard King
68. *The Adinkra Dictionary: A Visual Primer on The Language of ADINKRA* by W. Bruce Willis
69. *The Suppressed Rebellion: Black Revolution Conceived* by Areeb Malik Shabazz
70. *Maat: The 11 Laws of God* by Ra Un Nefer Amen
71. *Think and Grow Rich: A Black Choice* by Dennis Kimbro and Napoleon Hill
72. *The Twelve Universal Laws of Success* by Herbert Harris
73. *As a Man Thinketh* by James Allen

74. *The Prophet* by Kahlil Gibran
75. *Heal Thyself* by Queen Afua
76. *Sacred Woman* by Queen Afua
77. *African Holistic Health* by Llaila Afrika
78. *Drugs Masquerading as Food* by Suzar
79. *Blacked Out Through Whitewash* by Suzar
80. *The Africans Who Wrote the Bible* by Nana Banchie Darkwah
81. *The Deceiving of the Black Race* by Moses Farrar
82. *Enoch the Ethiopian: Lost Prophet of the Bible* by Indus Khamit-Kush
83. *Book of Coming Forth by Day: The Ethics of the Declarations of Innocence* by Maulana Karenga
84. *Selections from the Husia: Sacred Wisdom of Ancient Egypt* by Maulana Karenga
85. *Dr. John Henrik Clarke: His Life, His Words, His Works* by Anna Swanston
86. *Africans at the Crossroad: Notes for an African World Revolution* by John Henrik Clarke
87. *The Philosophy of Maat Kemetic-Soulism: Exposes Global European Imperialism* by Tep Maaxeru
88. *The Natural Blueprint for Relationships: Amanmere, Volume II* by Yao Nyamekye Morris
89. *Amanmere: The Natural Blueprint for Sexual Relationships* by Yao Nyamekye Morris
90. *Return to the African Mother Principle of Male and Female Equality* by Oba T'Shaka
91. *The United Independent Compensatory Code/System/Concept: A Textbook/Workbook for Thought, Speech and/or Action for Victims of Racism (White Supremacy)* by Neely Fuller Jr.
92. *The Art of Leadership, Volume 1 and 2* by Oba T'Shaka
93. *Spiritual Warriors Are Healers* by Mfundishi Jhutyms Ka N Heru Hassan K. Salim
94. *The Pale Fox* by Marcel Griaule and Germaine Dieterlen
95. *The Ruins of Empires* by C. F. Volney
96. *The Historical Jesus and the Mythical Christ* by Gerald Massey
97. *The Story of the Moors in Spain* by Stanley Lane-Poole
98. *Dalit: The Black Untouchables of India* by V. T. Rajshekar
99. *History of the First Council of Nice: A World's Christian Convention A.D. 325 with a Life of Constantine* by Dean Dudley
100. *A Right to be Hostile: The Boondocks Treasury* by Aaron McGruder

Recommended Fictional Reading:

1. *Not Without Laughter* by Langston Hughes
2. *The Best of Simple* by Langston Hughes
3. *Your Blues Ain't Like Mine* by Bebe Moore Campbell
4. *Brothers and Sisters* by Bebe Moore Campbell
5. *The Warmest December* by Bernice McFadden
6. *Family* by J. California Cooper
7. *No Man in the House* by Cecil Foster
8. *Slammin' Tar* by Cecil Foster
9. *Kindred* by Octavia Butler
10. *Tumbling* by Diane Mckinney-Whetstone
11. *Leaving Cecil Street* by Diane Mckinney-Whetstone
12. *Waiting in Vain* by Colin Channer
13. *Two Thousand Seasons* by Ayi Kwei Armah
14. *Invisible Man* by Ralph Ellison
15. *Native Son* by Richard Wright
16. *Jazz* by Toni Morrison
17. *Things Fall Apart* by Chinua Achebe
18. *A Gathering of Old Men* by Ernest J. Gaines
19. *A Lesson before Dying* by Ernest J. Gaines
20. Easy Rawlins Mysteries by Walter Mosley
21. Tamara Hayle Mysteries by Valerie Wilson Wesley
22. Coffin and Grave Digger Series by Chester Himes
23. *Black Girl Lost* by Donald Goines
24. Iceberg Slim Series by Iceberg Slims
25. *The Haunting of Hip Hop* by Bertrice Berry
26. *Midnight Robber* by Nalo Hopkinson
27. *My Soul to Keep* by Tanarive Due
28. The Vampire Huntress Series by L. A. Banks
29. *The Coldest Winter Ever* by Sister Souljah
30. *Blues for Mister Charlie* by James Baldwin

Recommended Books for Our Children:

1. *When I Look In the Mirror* by Sopoeia Greywolf
2. *Good Morning, Baby* by Cheryl Willis Hudson
3. *Good Night, Baby* by Cheryl Willis Hudson
4. *Let's Count, Baby* by Cheryl Willis Hudson
5. *Animal Sounds for Baby* by Cheryl Willis Hudson
6. *I Love My Hair!* by Natasha Anastasia Tarpley
7. *Afro-Bets Book of Color* by Cheryl Willis Hudson
8. *Afro-Bets Book of Number* by Cheryl Willis Hudson
9. *Afro-Bets Book of Letters* by Cheryl Willis Hudson
10. *Afro-Bets Book of Shapes* by Cheryl Willis Hudson
11. *Little Zeng's ABC's* by Acemandese Hall
12. *Afro-Tots Letters ABC* by Oswald J. Gift
13. *Afro-Tots Numbers 123* by Oswald J. Gift
14. *Please, Baby, Please* by Spike Lee
15. The Wonderful World of Myat Series by Omar Lewis
16. *Shades of Color* by Sandra L. Pinkney
17. *Whose Toes Are Those?* by Jabari Asim
18. *Whose Knees Are These?* by Jabari Asim
19. *Sweet, Sweet Baby* by Javaka Steptoe
20. *Golden Bear* by Ruth Young
21. *Nappy Hair* by Carolivia Herron
22. *Happy to Be Nappy* by Bell Hooks
23. *Five Notable Inventors* by Wade Hudson
24. *Five Bold Freedom Fighters* by Wade Hudson
25. *Five Brave Explorers* by Wade Hudson
26. *Five Brilliant Scientists* by Wade Hudson
27. *The Kids Book of Black Canadian History* by Rosemary Sadlier
28. *Africa* by Harriet Kinghorn
29. *Ellington was not a Street* by Ntozake Shange
30. *African Princess* by Joyce Hansen
31. *Anansi Does the Impossible: An Ashanti Tale* by Verna Aardema
32. *Her Stories: African American Folktales, Fairy Tales, and True Tales* by Virginia Hamilton
33. *The Girl Who Spun Gold* by Virginia Hamilton
34. *An Illustrated Treasury of African American Read-Aloud Stories* by Susan Kantor
35. *Uncle Remus The Complete Tales* by Julius Lester

36. *A Pride of African Tales* by Donna L. Washington
37. *African Beginnings* by James Haskins
38. *Portraits of African-American Heroes* by Tonya Bolden
39. *Let It Shine* by Andrea Davis Pinkney
40. *Kings and Queens of East Africa* by Anna Sylviane Diouf
41. Willimena Rules Series by Valerie Wilson Wesley
42. Carmen Browne Series by Stephanie Perry Moore
43. Payton Skky Series by Stephanie Perry Moore
44. Perry Skky Jr. Series by Stephanie Perry Moore
45. Drama High Series by L. Divine
46. *It Could Never Happen to Me* by Michelle Richards
47. *The Skin I'm In* by Sharon Flake
48. *Nzingha: Warrior Queen of Matamba Angola Africa 1595* by Patricia and Frederick Mckissack
49. *Philosophies of Life: Stories for Young People* by Kenneth Pollock
50. *Don't Give it Away!: A Workbook of Self Awareness and Self-Affirmations for Young Women* by Iyanla Vanzant

Recommendations for your DVD Collection:

1. *500 Years Later*
2. *Sankofa*
3. *Roots*
4. *What We Want, What We Believe: The Black Panther Party Library*
5. *Lumumba*
6. *Frederick Douglass: When the Lion Wrote History*
7. *Malcolm X Live*
8. *Shaka Zulu: The Complete Miniseries*
9. *African History vs. Biblical Myths, Part I and II* by Ashra Kwesi
10. *Sistahs in the Struggle, A Tribute to Black Women Liberators* by Merira Kwesi
11. *Post-Traumatic Slave Syndrome* by Dr. Joy DeGruy-Leary
12. *Black Wallstreet: An American Holocaust* by Jay Jay Wilson
13. *The Destruction of Black Civilization* and *African History* by Chancellor Williams and John G. Jackson
14. *A Great and Mighty Walk* by Dr. John Henrik Clarke
15. *Afrikan Spirituality and Psychiatry* by Richard King
16. *Africa: The Story of a Continent* by Basil Davidson
17. *Black Male and Female Relationship* by Dr. Amos Wilson
18. *Tell Me Who I Am*
19. *Our Friend, Martin*
20. *Kirikou*

Recommended Speeches, Lectures, and Interviews for Your Audio Collection:

1. *Afrikan People and European Holidays, Part 1 and 2* by Ishakamusa Barashango
2. *Message to the Bloods and Crips* by Minister Louis Farrakhan
3. Marcus Garvey Speaks by Marcus Garvey
4. *Who Were the Egyptians?* by Dr. Cheikh Anta Diop
5. *The Psychological Development of the Black Child* by Dr. Amos Wilson
6. *Christianity Before Christ* by John G. Jackson
7. *The Power of Images* by Dr. Na'Im Akbar
8. *Cultural Genocide in the Education System* by Dr. Yosef ben-Jochannan
9. *The Afrikan Foundations of World Knowledge* by Dr. Yosef ben-Jochannan
10. *The Great Empires of Ghana and Mali* by Dr. John Henrik Clarke
11. *The Concept of Race: An Evolving Issue* by Dr. John Henrik Clarke
12. Positive Action for Peace at the United Nations April 7, 1960, by Kwame Nkrumah
13. *Developing Positive Self-Images and Discipline in Black Children* by Dr. Jawanza Kunjufu
14. *A Call to Conscience: The Landmark Speeches of Dr. Martin Luther King Jr.*
15. *The African Power of Symbols* by Marimba Ani
16. *The Prison Industrial Complex* by Angela Davis
17. *Message to the Hip Hop Generation* by Sister Souljaj
18. *Circuits of the Brain* by Jewel Pookrum
19. *Socialism and the African American* by W. E. B. DuBois
20. *Reality of an Afrikan Holocaust* by Leonard Jeffries
21. Maurice Bishop Speaks
22. *Mutabaruka Interviewed* by Sankofaincipher
23. *African Historiography* by Jacob Carruthers
24. *The Struggle of the Working Class* by Walter Rodney
25. *Race First* by Chancellor Williams

References List

1. Wade W. Nobles. (2006). *Seeking the Sakhu*. Chicago: Third World Press.
2. Maurice Bishop. (1983). *Maurice Bishop Speaks : The Grenada Revolution and its Overthrow 1979-83*. New York: Pathfinder.
3. Amy Jacques Garvey. (1986). *The Philosophy & Opinions of Marcus Garvey or, Africa for the Africans*. Massachusetts: The Majority Press.
4. Ishakamusa Barashango. (1991). *Afrikan Genesis : Amazing Stories of Man's Beginnings*. Washington, D.C.: IVth Dynasty Publishing Company.
5. Dr. Frances Cress Welsing. (1991). *The Isis Papers : The Keys to the Colors*. Washington, D.C.: C.W. Publishing
6. Haile Selassie I. (2000). *Selected Speeches of HIS Imperial Majesty Haile Selassie I*. New York : One Drop Books
7. Amos Wilson. (1998). *Blueprint for Black Power : A Moral, Political, and Economic Imperative for the Twenty-First Century*. New York : Afrikan World Book Distributor
8. Kwame Agyei & Akua Nson Akoto. (2000). *The Sankofa Movement: Reafrikanization & the Reality of War*. Washington, D.C.) yoko InfoCom Inc.
9. Asa G. Hilliard III. (1998). *SBA: The Reawakening of the African Mind*. Florida: Makare Publishing Company.
10. Na'im Akbar. (1991). *Visions for Black Men*. Florida: Mind Productions & Associates, Inc.
11. Sobonfu Somé. (1997). *The Spirit of Intimacy : Ancient African Teachings in the Ways of Relationships*. New York : Harpercollins.
12. Robin Walker. (2006). *When We Ruled*. London : Every Generation Media.
13. Chancellor Williams. (1987). *The Destruction of Black Civilization : Great Issues of a Race from 4500 B.C. to 2000 A.D*. Chicago: Third World Press.
14. Areeb Malik Shabazz. (2002). *The Suppressed Rebellion : Black Revolution Conceived*. Charlotte: Conquering Books, LLC.
15. Janet Cheatham Bell. (1997). *Inspiring Quotations for Entrepreneurs : The Soul of Success*. New York: John Wiley & Sons, Inc.

16. Janet Cheatham Bell. (1990). *Famous Black Quotations On Women, Love and Other Topics.* Chicago: Sabayt Publications, Inc.

17. Quinn Eli. (1997). *Many Strong and Beautiful Voices : Quotations from Africans Throughout the Diaspora.* Philadelphia: Running Press.

18. Terri L. Jewell. (1993). *The Black Woman's Gumbo Ya-Ya.* California: The Crossing Press.

19. Danielle and Olivier Follmi. (2005). *Origins : African Wisdom for Every Day.* New York: Harry N. Abrams, Inc.

20. Teishan Latner. (2005). *The Quotable Rebel: Political Quotations for Dangerous Times.* Maine: Common Courage Press.

21. Julia Stewart. (2005). *Stewart's Quotable African Women.* New York: Penguin Books.

22. Julia Stewart. (1997). *African Proverbs and Wisdom: A Collection for Every Day of the Year, From More Than Forty African Nations.* New Jersey: A Citadel Press Book.

23. Patrick Ibekwe. (1998). *Wit & Wisdom of Africa : Proverbs from Africa & the Caribbean.* England: New Internationalist Publications Ltd.

24. Wade Hudson. (2004). *Powerful Words : More Than 200 Years of Extraordinary Writing By African Americans.* New York: Scholastic Inc.

25. Baruti K. Kafele. (1991). *A Black Parent's Handbook to Educating Your Children (Outside of the Classroom).* New Jersey: Baruti Publishing.

26. Kahlil Gibran. (2005). *The Kahlil Gibran Reader: Inspirational Writings.* New York: Kensington Publishing Corp.

27. Kahlil Gibran. (2005). *Love Letters in the Sand: The Love Poems of Khalil Gibran.* London: Souvenir Press.

28. Hugh S. Williamson. (2003). Soul Adventurer . . . *Passages from Life.* Brampton: Hueman Xpress.

29. Oba T'Shaka. (1990). *The Art of Leadership Volume I.* California: Pan Afrikan Publications.

30. Alex Haley. (1965). *The Autobiography of Malcolm X.* New York: Ballantine Books.

31. Ngũgĩ Wa Thiong'O. (1986). *Decolonising the Mind: The Politics of Language in African Literature.* New Hampshire: Heinemann.

32. Elijah Muhammad. (1997). *Message to the Blackman in America.* Missouri: Secretarius MEMPS Ministries.

33. Carter G. Woodson. (2000). *The Mis-Education of The Negro.* Chicago: African American Images.

34. Tony Martin. (1986). *Message to the People: The Course of African Philosophy.* Massachusetts: The Majority Press.

35. John S Mbiti. (1969). *African Religions and Philosophy*. New Hampshire: Heinemann.
36. Les Brown. (1997). *It's Not Over Until You Win!*. New York: Simon & Schuster.
37. Iyanla Vanzant. (1993). *Acts of Faith: Daily Meditations for People of Color*. New York: Simon & Schuster.
38. Muata Ashby. (1996). *Egyptian Proverbs: Mystical Wisdom Teachings and Meditations*. Florida: Cruzian Mystic Books.
39. James Allen. (2004). *The Wisdom of James Allen III*. California: Laurel Creek Press.
40. James Allen. (2003) *The Wisdom of James Allen II*. California: Laurel Creek Press.
41. James Allen (2001) *The Wisdom of James Allen: 5 Classic Works Combined Into One*. California: Laurel Creek Press.
42. Anna Swanston. (2003). *Dr. John Henrik Clarke—His Life His Words His Work*. Georgia: I AM Unlimited Publishing.
43. James L. Conveyers, Jr & Julius E. Thompson. *The Life and Times of John Henrik Clarke*. (2004). New Jersey: African World Press, Inc.
44. Anthony Ephirim-Donker. (1997). *African Spirituality: On Becoming Ancestors*. New Jersey: African World Press, Inc.
45. Foundation For Inner Peace. (1992). *A Course In Miracles*. California: Foundation For Inner Peace.
46. Na'im Akbar. (1998). *Know Thy Self*. Florida: Mind Productions & Associates Inc.
47. Chogyam Trungpa. (1998) *Shambhala: The Sacred Path of the Warrior*. Boston: Shambhala.
48. Robert Fleming. (1996). *The Wisdom of the Elders: A Wealth of Inspiritional Quotations from the Speeches and Writings of Some of Black America's Most Esteemed Men and Women*. New York: Ballantine Books
49. Keith Harrell. (2003). *Attitude is Everything: 10 Life-Changing Steps to Turning Attitude into Action*. New York: HarperCollins.
50. Dennis Kimbro. (2005). *What Keeps Me Standing: Letters from Black Grandmothers on Peace, Hope, and Inspiration*. New York: Harlem Moon.
51. Jawanza Kunjufu. (1991). *Black Economics: Solutions for Economic and Community Empowerment*. Chicago: African American Images.
52. *Handbook for the New Paradigm*. Nevada: Bridger House Publishers, Inc.
53. William H. T. Baily. (2000). *Building a Healthy Sense of Self: Essential Knowledge for African People*. Philadelphia: Baily Publishing

A Special Thanks to

The family of Asa G. Hillard III
The Majority Press
Na'im Akbar
Wade Nobles
Frances Cess Welsing
Kwame Agyei and Akua Nson
HIS Imperial Majesty Haile Selassie I
Maurice Bishop
Martin Luther King
Marcus Garvey
Malcolm X
Amos N. Wilson
Asa G. Hilliard III
Ishakamusa Barashango
Chancellor Williams
Robin Walker
Langston Hughes
Carolette Liburd
Michele Liburd
Francis Mclean
Kevin Jones
Kofi Sankofa
Annison and Hugh
Derrick Williams
Winston Small

Sean Liburd is the founder and co-owner of Knowledge Bookstore: a celebration of the wondrous achievements of Africans and their descendants worldwide. He is an entrepreneur, a Pan-African, a community builder, a listener, a thinker, and a visionary. As a valued member of the Knowledge Bookstore family, he is committed to providing the tools to promote racial and cultural pride and is dedicated to learning, sharing and teaching the true history of Africans worldwide.

You are invited to "come-union" with Sean at *communion@knowledgebookstore. com* or *www.knowledgebookstore.com*